# The Proximity Factor

## Essential Disciplines in a Leader's Spiritual Formation

Jim Beaird

PUBLISHING

ISBN: 1500536628
ISBN-13: 978-1500536626

# DEDICATION

I'd like to thank Kris, my best friend and wife, for believing in me and sharing the journey to this project's completion. Thank you Drs. Wayne and Sherry Lee for encouraging me to take the next step in my personal leadership development. A special thanks to my dear friend, Dr. Paul Leavenworth, for his encouragement and guidance.

Thank you, Drs. Nick and Leona Venditti for planting the seeds of the dream I now live. Thank you, Ken Groen, for teaching me how to pace myself for the long haul.

And to my mother, Dorothy, who invested her life in prayerful partnership for her children. I could always count on your prayers!

# CONTENTS

# INTRODUCTION

---

*"If the ax is dull, and one does not sharpen the edge, then he must use more strength; But wisdom brings success."* Ecclesiastes 10:10

---

There is an old saying that asks, "Why work hard when you can work smart?" We generally do not experience a loss for things to do. Appointments, schedules, commitments, etc., demand our attention and drain our energy away from serving the lord with all our heart.

When our personal ax gets dull we lose efficiency and effectiveness. Its sharp cutting-edge offensive usually yields to a maintenance existence that robs us of creativity and growth. *We spend time applying bandages rather than good judgment.* A subtle relationship with the mistress of "second-best" robs us of our first love and clouds our perspective.

A personal inventory *should* reveal the condition of our ax's edge. From time to time we must inspect the cutting edge. If it is dull, we can continue to work at what we're doing, but with less efficiency and much more effort. Dull edges produce blistered hands and sore backs and exponentially compound the difficulty of the task. Additionally, those to whom we minister eventually feel the effects of our lack of maintenance.

Where is the fine line that divides a strong and healthy work ethic from a diseased and misapplied concept of productivity? The answer lies in the need for individual and corporate times of revitalization—a renewing of vision and a refreshing of intent.

The revitalization of our lives and ministries insures more effectiveness and less "down-time." The lack of joy in our lives generally characterizes the impact of allowing the cutting edge

1

to dull. More strength is required to accomplish what was once easy. A sense of drudgery often replaces the joy of service to the Lord. Then, in the midst of our misery, we make decisions that alter God's plan—simply based on our perspective of His intent in our lives. Misplaced priorities and unfruitful activities brought us to this very point wherein we try to decide just how we will let God continue to "lead" us in the calling we once felt so honored to receive.

This book does not dispense theory. Everything within the pages of this book derives from years of walking through God's plan for my life and what I had to realize if I intended to finish well. I provided both a real-life narrative dealing with the pressures and pain of developing spiritual disciplines and a sound theology to guide that process. As I point out in greater detail within the following chapters, what a man or woman does in private determines what he or she becomes in public.

I deal with issues germane to ministry and the spiritual leader's intentionality in developing a life pattern that incorporates the disciplines of solitude, sabbatical, solidarity, and the resultant strategy that comes from having been in close proximity to the Father's heart. The illustration of a sharp ax edge provides a worthy word picture of the leader's self-management. Periodic maintenance changes the whole picture. Increased attention to one's personal time with the Father and how to maximize that time greatly increases ministry productivity and diminishes ministry burnout and failure.

Dr. Jim Beaird

CHAPTER 1

# The Story Behind The Story: *Our* Story

*While ministry had initially been enjoyable, it now weighed like a ton of bricks in the backpack of duty and performance.*

I felt like my hands had been duct-taped to the treadmill of thankless duty. Every day became an exercise in survival. The prospect of successful ministry seemed distant and improbable. My concept of what successful ministry was supposed to entail had evaporated—only to be replaced by disillusionment. Pessimism replaced optimism as the filter through which I began to see everything related to ministry and the church. While ministry had initially been enjoyable, it now weighed like a ton of bricks in the backpack of duty and performance.

My early mentors modeled a driven style of ministry wherein they spent every waking moment serving the ministry. They all used slogans with pride that declared they would labor long and hard for the Kingdom—even if it cost them their lives. Some did and some died. Their workaholic approach to ministry became the template I used to form my own work ethic. After all, I didn't want anyone to think that ministers didn't earn their keep! I remember spending every night of the week away from my wife because I worked with a pastor who never took a day off to recharge. We spent every night calling on prospective members or conducting Bible studies for the church. Saturdays were spent either calling on rural families needing a ride on the church bus the next morning or practicing the music for Sunday's services.

One day I received a call from a district superintendent in another state. He painted the picture of potential of a certain church in a small town that only needed the "right pastor" to lead them and love them. We've all heard that before. I've since realized that the word "potential" is the best bait to catch unwitting young ministers wanting to follow God's plan for their life. I accepted the call to the rural setting and began the move across three state lines. The process involved giving up several things we valued so we could fit into the new ministry scenario. We thought that by paring

---

*We had become the solution to someone else's problem. With our appointment to the church, we heard very little from the superintendent. His job was done and ours was just beginning.*

---

back on personal possessions we would be better able to live in the meager setting that awaited us. Sacrifice. That's what the mentors said. "If we are to be effective in the ministry, we need to be willing to give up everything and live with whatever the church provides." I'm sure there's some rationale in that statement, but in retrospect, I'm also sure we missed its true meaning. When we arrived, we were given a different story than the superintendent had given us. The church had no means by which to pay us or support us financially. We were young and willing to do whatever was necessary to get established in this great calling. We had become the solution to someone else's problem. With our appointment to the church, we heard very little from the superintendent. His job was done and ours was just beginning.

Adjustment to our new surroundings rapidly caused the luster of the "opportunity" to fade. Having burned certain bridges and sold our valued possessions, we set about carving something out of nothing. The next three years saw the acquisition of property and a building program in which I felt that I was the only one who was committed enough to stay the course and establish a place to worship for this church.

On one particular day, I had an appointment with a banker to inquire about accessibility to a loan with which we could finance our building program. That appointment had to be postponed an hour, so I used the time until then to visit a sporting goods store on the edge of town. The fishing gear covered an entire wall. A store clerk waited until I picked up a fly rod and then asked if there was anything he could do to help me. Small talk ensued, and then he asked what I did for a job. I proudly told him that I was a pastor. His response played a major role in influencing how I began to perceive my role as a minister. He said, "Oh, a pastor . . . you must get to fish four or five days a week." It bothered me that he thought ministers had all week to play around and only had to work an hour a week. That reinforced my already twisted sense of what I thought God wanted from me in ministry. I felt like I already modeled the work ethic engrained in me from an early age by my father. Yet, something clicked in my mind at that very moment and I determined that I would prove him wrong. I would work harder than anyone else and nobody could ever say that Jim Beaird was just a lazy preacher.

Subsequent venues for ministry opportunities always required that I work outside of the church to support myself. Seventeen of the first thirty years of ministry involved being bi-vocational. While we knew that planting churches required much personal sacrifice, we grew more disenchanted with ministry with every year that passed. Why did God demand so much of us? We responded to His call on our lives, yet, seemingly, we had to pay our own way. As our little family grew to include three boys, it became increasingly difficult to plant a church, work a full-time job, and raise children with a healthy perspective of God and what He demands of our lives. In those early years of ministry, we did not have the resources available to church planters today. We simply dug in, worked our hardest, and left the rest with God.

We were in our late thirties. We successfully planted a church that became the fastest growing church in the county. The state economy took a major hit with the oil recession of the eighties and the high rate of inflation. Seventy-two hundred homes in the area went into foreclosure and our church plant was hit especially hard. Church income dropped drastically and the church board had to lay off the secretary and cut my salary in half in order to stay financially solvent. I again resorted to working outside the church to make ends meet. My optimistic outlook once again dimmed as I began to sense that God must actually have a plan to keep me broke and tired. At that point, I didn't care. I struggled to keep a positive mindset as I felt like I had no power over the quicksand that was pulling me downward. I felt the guilt of those feelings and kept telling myself that God would come through and we would come out the other side of this difficult time with a great testimony of how God supplied at the last minute. However, the provision never seemed to come as I began to seriously question my call to ministry.

I married my high school sweetheart. We both spent our teenage years in the same church and participated in the youth group. We dated for five years before getting married in college. We determined to honor each other and save ourselves for marriage. We often prayed together on dates. We did everything right—by the book. We had no regrets of any sinful activity nor did we ever question God's call on our lives together into ministry. Now, in our late thirties, we began to question everything about what we had always felt was God's leading in our lives. I saw less of my family because of the recession and need for secular employment. All joy in what we were supposed to be called of God to do had evaporated.

My secular employment involved doing law enforcement for a community just north of where I lived. I worked the midnight shift and struggled to sleep in the daytime. I came home from work one particular morning and sat on the edge of my bed. As I sat there, I tried to gather thoughts and regain perspective. I remember a deep depression descending over me as I began to wonder if things would ever change. My youngest son played in the driveway as I sat and pondered my next decision. I took my revolver out of its holster and thought that just one quick pull of the trigger and I would never be tired again. It would be so easy and quick. Just then, I heard a child's laughter coming from the driveway. I looked out my second-story window and discovered the source of unfettered joy. My son was playing on his Big Wheel and having the time of his life. He would coast down the driveway, then, at the last moment before hitting the curb, crank his handlebars hard to one side— causing a "spinout." He had no way of knowing, but his laughter was for me very timely. I snapped back to reality and replaced the gun in its holster. As I look back on those events, I realize they were all a part of God's plan to draw me close to his heart and to impart something that could help others who struggle with His master plan for their lives. The only cure for weary leadership is proximity—to the heart of the father.

I began to understand that a college degree and a few years of ministry experience had neither prepared me for the avalanche of expectations nor equipped me to lead spiritually within the context of ministry God had chosen for my life. I soon found that time spent on my knees trumped time learning theories and styles of ministry. God wanted only to communicate with me and reveal His great love as He guided me through difficult times and began developing character qualities needed to see me through His call into a life-long commitment to ministry.

Retrospect tells me that everything I needed to persevere and succeed in ministry came from time spent alone with God as He patiently led me through misguided perceptions of what ministry was supposed to be and what it actually entailed. I realized I could not succeed at ministry until I succeeded at the disciplines necessary to build a strong spiritual base. Expertise and elevated skill levels can take a leader only so far—still short of God's design. Before I could effectively lead others, I had to lead myself in the spiritual disciplines from which the revelation of God's plan for my life came.

I shared my story because I suspect I am not alone in the assertion that many—maybe even most—leaders go through a season of life in which everything they once believed in or held as a personal conviction gets tested to the breaking point. I intend to share essential disciplines of effective leadership that operate *only* in close proximity to the Father's heart.

# CHAPTER 2

# Substitutes for Anointing

---

*"But you have an anointing from the Holy One, and you know all things."* 1 John 2:20

---

The enemy of our soul seeks to replicate everything God wants to impart to us as weapons of warfare, words of direction and guidance, and power for life and ministry. If he can get us to avoid using God's power to defeat him, he deals a setback to us in our quest to impose the rule of God's kingdom in our lives. He has many substitutes for God's anointing and subtly allows us to pursue a particular path or mission in the strength we've grown accustomed to using— except it is usually not the anointing of God.

The Proximity Factor describes the essential disciplines for effective leadership. But prior to that discussion, we need to know that true anointing comes only from time spent with the Father. This chapter discusses several possible substitutes for that anointing.

## Charisma:

A common substitute for God's anointing is charisma. That word implies a personality-driven characteristic that imbues the possessor with a natural ability to lead. People like to be around charismatic personalities because they personify everything typical of the individual capable of leading.

The denotation of charisma as a substitute for true anointing does not negate its potential for the kingdom of God if used within the context of Spirit-led activity. It simply means that charismatic individuals tend to rely on that natural gift to motivate other individuals and to influence decision-making. The leader who resorts to the yardstick of his own personality usually comes up short when times demand a well-thought-out and prayerful decision affecting the well being of those he seeks to lead.

Charisma, by its very name, implies a gift of persuasion and influence. Those who fail to honor God with this gift will likely develop shortcuts through their personal spiritual formation. Their tendency to rely upon their powers of influence can replace the anointing that comes only from time spent listening to the Father in solitude. It's almost as if they say, "I got this, God," and continue down the path of self-revelation but fail to reflect the wisdom or perspective of God. Persuasiveness becomes the hammer used to nail down the message or convince others of the logical course of action.

Charisma is not evil in and of itself. It can only be used by the enemy of our soul if it becomes a *substitute* for having drawn close to the Father's heart and received His impartation of wisdom and guidance. Wisdom gained in proximity to the Father's heart always reflects His power because it reflects His intention to fortify and equip those He calls and to whom He reveals the fruit of solitude. What comes out of solitude always trumps misguided charisma.

## Style (public speaking ability):

Most leaders desire to be effective speakers. Perhaps their decision to develop that component of their ministry came from having to listen to less-than-inspiring pastors who did not have a clue about what effective communication was all about. Perhaps they heard an evangelist or speaker who held them in rapt attention for the entirety of the sermon and who could paint an unforgettable picture in words. Regardless of their intent to refine their speaking ability, those who desire to become apt communicators usually accomplish their goal.

The danger comes in the subtle reliance upon persuasive speech that did not find its origin in the Father's heart. Rather than relying upon the Holy Spirit to anoint the message, many leaders fall into the subtle temptation to rely on the dynamics of their delivery or style. I love great preachers and I can tell when a preacher has spent time with the Father. Simple messages become profound and gentle words become powerful. I can also tell when the delivery means more than the message. While I believe that God expects us to develop the mechanics of our delivery, I also believe that He desires to impart the power that will ultimately drive the words into the hearts of anticipating believers and skeptical non-believers.

Delivery style shapes the listening habits of the audience. Depending on the quality of the delivery, it also shapes the level of expectation toward other speakers. A congregation that has enjoyed a dynamic style of delivery often gauges new pastoral candidates by the style of the out-going pastor.

---

*Delivery style shapes the listening habits of the audience.*

---

The revered style becomes the template by which they evaluate the public speaking component of a new pastor's ability to lead a public service. The congregation often missed the heart message of the Father because they became dependent on the persuasive and dynamic delivery style of the former minister. Their acceptance of the message came from cleverly linked words and thoughts delivered in an evangelistic (and often demonstrative) style. Each sermon adhered to the expectancy level of the listeners and not the still small voice of the Holy Spirit. Its effect is subtle but effective in elevating style over substance gained from time spent in private with the Father.

Some leaders miss the mark because the public gift takes priority over the private discipline. They spend hours perfecting the ability to produce a "good sound" when God is really only interested in a "sound heart." From that sound heart comes the power of persuasion that transforms the hearts of men and women hungry for the authentic impartation of a God jealous for their attention. I know the temptation to trust in preparation and delivery and I know the power and effectiveness that comes only from time spent listening to the Father.

## Intelligence:

We dare not rely on heightened intelligence as a substitute for anointing. While God encourages individuals to develop their intelligence, He also provides the foundation for understanding things not of human origin. Intelligence has the potential for disconnect from the message being given if the lines of communication get severed by a speaker intent on living within a menagerie of fluffy-feathered words and concepts. Many remember the struggle to understand the concept the speaker tried to convey but came away confused from the perplexity of the topic's presentation.

God is not against intelligence. He gave us the ability to gain knowledge and available wisdom to use it correctly.

However, the simplicity of the Gospel provides common ground by which all can come to repentance and live in the transformation the Gospel affords. Sermons do not need to become an exercise in academia in order to present the facts of the gospel capable of influencing a person's decision to follow Christ. The simple presentation of the Good News confounds the profundity of a message laced with words that impress but do not transform thinking.

## Influence:

Some people have more influence than others—for whatever reason. Every church has people who carry influence in key decisions. For instance, a pastor or leader can insert influence to guide couples through difficult stages in their marriages. However, influence can also direct people away from God's will. When used as a substitute for anointing, influence imposes man's will where God's will should prevail. Influence should be the reflection of Godly wisdom and not the imposition of a personal preference.

Every pastor or leader knows that most congregations have "influence brokers" who know their influence carries more weight than the average church member. Whether or not they use their influence appropriately, they still know their influence is an uncommon commodity that has the potential to chart the course of a church.

When the pastor is the main influencer in the church setting, the temptation is the same. He or she knows that their influence, when imposed upon a congregation, has the power to either produce personal preference in a situation or to reflect insight and wisdom gained from proximity to the Father's heart. That does not mean that personal preference is wrong. It simply means that it *can* be wrong if it is a substitute for time with the Father. Everyone must eventually give an account of how they use influence.

## Connectedness (who you know):

An individual who knows someone in a place of influence who can make a quick call or referral usually gains the inside track in securing a position or pastorate desired. Most leaders are well connected and utilize the network system for making or gaining professional appointments. However, connectedness in this context refers to an individual's reliance upon someone having authority or influence to gain him or her a position in a church and does not necessarily include the counsel gained in the Father's presence. That is the system.

We need references to move through the maze of life. But when an individual gains a position solely on someone else's reputation, that individual often fails to rightly discern God's plan for his or her life. Perhaps a certain family has had several generations of ministers—all who have had successful ministry. The name recognition often provides an unfair advantage to the relative over the list of other applicants. That is not a bad thing, but it can become a reason for not developing an intimate audience with the Father.

## Routine:

When an individual first enters ministry, they gather materials and file templates that hopefully will serve them later during times of public ministry. As time goes by, they become less and less dependent upon those templates and rather begin to rely upon their own methods of performing a certain task. They use what works and discard what does not apply to their particular ministry need.

While they once sought God's influence in their decision making, they evolve to a self-sufficiency that neither requires God's direction nor does it actively seek His blessing. Sadly, ministry becomes a predictable exercise in familiar methodology. Most pastors and ministry leaders can identify with this familiar propensity to replace effectiveness with efficiency in lieu of actually seeking the anointing of the Father. After all, there are some things we learn to do very well and require little rethinking. However, when public ministry conforms to the template of predictability and ease of execution, the anointing cannot break the yolk of sin that enslaves the majority of faithful congregants.

Routine in daily matters is one thing. But the routine that avoids the personal spiritual discipline of seeking the Father's heart is another. Pastors get so "dug in" that they cannot rightly discern the issues that require input from close proximity to the Father's heart. In so avoiding that divine influence, they position themselves for eventual burnout or failure or both.

Everyone loves predictable routine. It makes the job easier and usually gives a track upon which to get from one place to another. The ministry is full of tasks that need to get done. However, the danger comes in allowing the mindless execution of tasks to define how we interpret Scripture or how we deliver what we claim to be the message for the hour. If it is the product of a preparatory routine it will never touch a single heart with power capable to transform it. Make no mistake. Routine can be a subtle substitute for the anointing.

## First-Century Vignettes

The Apostle Paul receives credit for having written thirteen of the New Testament books and conducted missionary journeys that introduced the Gospel to several countries. However, the beginning of his spiritual formation included revelations from God that shaped his entire perspective of who he was and who he was to become.

The first vignette we have of Paul's gradual transformation into the leader God could effectively use is recorded in Galatians 1 and takes place around 49 A.D. Paul was quick to assert himself as an Apostle who received what he had directly from God in Arabia and not from man. He mentioned going up to Jerusalem and confronting some of the other Apostles—even to withstand Peter face to face. He overtly inferred that he should be placed at the top of the apostle's list with Peter. Perhaps his previous position in the secularly controlled religious establishment still clouded his personal perspective. His heart had changed but his mind still viewed the cataclysmic events leading to his conversion as events associated with importance—a role he had played for years as he sought out and persecuted the early Christians. It is possible for a man to have a change of heart and still hold to a well-established self-concept of social preeminence. Such a concept holds the probability of abandonment of the new and return to the familiar.

The second vignette of Paul takes place about seven years later. As recorded in 1 Corinthians 15:9, he admitted that he was the *least* of the apostles. Having already endured countless hardships and multiple instances of resistance to the message he proclaimed, he gains a different spirit. It was during this time that the transformation took place that would prove to be transformational in his dependence upon God.

Five years later, Ephesians 3:8 records his sentiment in the third vignette of Paul's spiritual development as he declares, "I am the least of all saints!" He credited God with having given him the grace to preach the Gospel of Jesus Christ among the Gentiles. As he ministered to and lived among the converts in the young church, he saw that his credentials meant nothing of significance in his new role as missionary to the people he formerly persecuted. They had remained steadfast in their faith and actually assisted him in the development of his ministry gifts. He recognized their incredible impact upon his trajectory as the leader God would use greatly.

The final vignette of revelation to Paul came four or five years later as He shared with Timothy, "This is a faithful saying...Christ came into the world to save sinners, of whom I am chief," (1 Tim. 1:15). Paul went from being the self-proclaimed leading apostle to the chief of sinners. That is quite a transformation—both in terms of self-perception and usability by God. Before God could effectively use Paul, He had to strip away anything that Paul relied upon as a substitute for true anointing. While he had significant attributes of leadership in the human realm, they availed him nothing in the spiritual realm until he yielded them to God.

Paul's progression into usability by God went from the *top* of the Apostles list to becoming the *least* of the apostles. Then, he declared himself to be at the *bottom* of the Christians list and at the *top* of the sinners list. An effective leader must value on-going personal transformation. Only leaders who count and pay the cost of such change emerge capable of leading and overseeing the leadership development of those they lead. Paul gained a proper perspective, both in terms of his personal transformation and the possibilities of any individual completely dependent upon God's favor and anointing to accomplish mission for God.

Paul finally emerged with no reliance upon his previously held "substitutes" for God's anointing. But to become the catalyst for God's Kingdom that he ultimately became, he had to lay down everything he formerly depended upon and learn anew the source of his authority and power for impacting his world in an entirely different manner. He learned the secret of Proximity to the Father's Heart.

# CHAPTER 3

# Proximity To The Father's Heart

*When the Spirit of God intersects with the human spirit, a radical sense of God's presence rewrites the script of the leader's expectancy of Him.*

An effective leader must value on-going personal transformation. Personal change leading to transformation requires self-discipline and great sacrifice. Only leaders who count and pay the cost of such change emerge capable of leading and overseeing the leadership development of those they lead. "One key to successful leadership is continuous personal change... a reflection of our inner growth and empowerment. Empowered leaders are the only ones who can induce real change."[1] Leaders who do not experience personal change have not experienced sufficient time in proximity to the Father's heart and therefore cannot lead effectively in the current culture; neither can they facilitate

---

[1] James M. Kouzes, *Business Leadership: A Jossey-Bass Reader* (San Francisco: Jossey-Bass, 2003), 522.

change in the lives of leaders they oversee. Proximity is simply the relative position of one object (or person) to another. Merriam Webster defines "proximity" as, "the quality or state of being proximate: closeness."[2] God's will cannot be known by leaders who desire to lead with effectiveness and authenticity yet fail to remain in proximity to His heart.

Prior to the Apostle Paul's emergence as the leader he eventually became, a time of personal transformation necessitated by God's intersection with his life set the course for both heightening his spiritual awareness and development of his gifts and resident skills. Paul did not set out to change his life into something God might deem worthy of His approval. Rather, God's unexpected interruption into the course of his life initiated the process of transformation necessary before any effectiveness could surface. "To put it bluntly: the whole leadership thing is a demented concept. Leaders are neither born nor made. Leaders are summoned. They are called into existence by circumstances. Those who rise to the occasion are leaders."[3] God summoned Paul in an unconventional manner at an inconvenient time (Acts 9:1-9). That singular event started a chain reaction in a leader whose life became God's template for the first-century Church.

Paul's transformation electrified the Primitive Church as the comparison between his old life and his transformed life fueled both controversy and reluctant acceptance. He had great difficulty reconciling the deeds of his past with what appeared to be his future course. Such comparison often drives the leader to a state of self-contemplation in which the

---

[2] *The Merriam-Webster Dictionary*, s.v. "Proximity."
[3] Leonard Sweet, *Summoned to Lead* (Grand Rapids: Zondervan, 2004), 12.

remnants of the old life seek to disqualify the leader from embracing the truth of the new life. "When in honesty we accept the evil that is in us as part of the truth about ourselves and offer that truth up to God, we are in a mysterious way nourished. Even the truth about our shadow side sets us free."[4] Paul diffused the accusations associated with previous endeavor and eventually shifted his mindset to assimilate the immensity of the mission before him. He realized that a change had, indeed, taken place and that he was no longer responsible for his previous deeds against the Church, but had become the steward of a calling and a catalyst to precipitate change necessary for the proclamation of the gospel message.

His theology of leadership launched a personal life-long journey to find the Father's heart and go there often. "When we set a goal of any type, that goal presupposes that a journey of sorts must be undertaken."[5] He aimed both to model and to proclaim the transformed life and to embark upon a journey designed by God to demonstrate His great love to all nations. Paul's change became apparent to all who made it past their initial dismissal of Paul's mission. They witnessed the effects of a profound change that became both Paul's battle cry throughout his remaining life and his challenge to the world he determined to reach with the truth of God's love and the message of hope for all humankind.

Such a transformation demands continual adaptation and course correction. Paul's heavenly mandate did not include personal choices or preferences as to the recipients of his

---

[4] Richard J. Foster, *Prayer: Finding the Heart's True Home* (New York: HarperCollins, 1992), 31.

[5] Samuel D. Rima, *Leading from the Inside Out: The Art of Self-Leadership* (Grand Rapids: Baker Books, 2000), 85.

message of hope and transformation. He says, "...to the weak I became as weak, that I might win the weak. I have become all things to all men, that I might by all means save some" (1 Cor. 9:22).[6] It became necessary to lay down his preconceptions in lieu of missional effectiveness. "In pursuing deep change, we redesign our maps or paradigms and realign ourselves with our surrounding environment. We reinvent ourselves by changing our perspective."[7] Mission becomes the template into which the leader must fit as the retooling of ministry gifts and reframing of ministry context takes precedence over conventionality and familiar methodology. However, mission can only be rightly discerned if the leader mandates in his or her life the disciplines associated with gaining the presence of the Father and hearing His heart.

The entire premise of gaining the presence of the Father's heart begins with the understanding that discipline and intentionality drive the effort. The desired effect gained from that effort provides a template by which an effective leader continually gains the Father's presence and rightly discerns the Father's desire and how it can play out in the leader's life and ministry. Isaiah prophesied the restoration of the Messianic Kingdom when he said, "The Spirit of the Lord shall rest upon him, the spirit of wisdom and understanding, the spirit of counsel and might, the spirit of knowledge and of the fear of the Lord" (Isa. 11:2). While the import of the prophetic verse aligns itself with the Messianic eschatology to come, the essence of the passage also applies to the leader

---

[6] All Scriptural quotes, unless otherwise noted, are from the New King James Version.

[7] Robert E. Quinn, *Deep Change: Discovering the Leader Within* (San Francisco: Jossey-Bass, 1996), 66.

who seeks to position himself or herself in close proximity to the Father's heart.

The Celtic Prayer postulates the possibility of a changed heart from having been in the presence of the Father. "O Son of God, perform a miracle for me; change my heart. You, whose crimson blood redeems mankind, whiten my heart. It is you who makes the sun bright and the ice sparkle; you who makes the rivers flow and the salmon leap. Your skilled hand makes the nut tree blossom, and the corn turn golden; your spirit composes the songs of the birds and the buzz of the bees. Your creation is a million wondrous miracles, beautiful to behold. I ask of you just one more miracle: beautify my soul."[8]

Only when God touches the human heart can real change—or even transformation—take place. The human heart that invites God's redeeming touch experiences what no human agency can offer. When the Spirit of God intersects with the human spirit, a radical sense of God's presence rewrites the script of the leader's expectancy of Him. A familiar and comforting presence replaces the hurried and harried activity surrounding life and ministry. The Psalmist rightly declares, "The Lord is my strength and my shield; my heart trusts in Him and I am helped. My heart leaps for joy and I will give thanks to Him in song" (Ps. 28:7) and, "I have chosen the way of truth; I have set my heart on Your laws" (119:30).

After David's moral failure with Bathsheba, David cries out to God imploring Him to, "create in me a pure heart, O God, and renew a steadfast spirit within me" (51:10). He did not desire to lose the power of God's presence in his life. The

---

[8] Mel Lawrenz, *The Dynamics of Spiritual Formation*, Ministry Dynamics for a New Century Series (Grand Rapids: Baker Books, 2000), 29.

association of the terms "clean," "heart," "new," and "spirit," calls to mind Ezekiel 36:25-27, which also testifies to God's willingness to forgive and ability to re-create. The repetition of the word "spirit" (*ruah*) in verses 10-12 reinforces this message.[9] David's brokenness revealed the heart of a loving Father who sought only to restore and redeem. Proximity to that heart became David's life theme as he found himself calling out to the Father whenever he sensed a developing distance. "But on this one will I look: On him who is poor and of a contrite spirit, and who trembles at My word" (Isa. 66:2). "The Father affirms his attention to a particular kind of person: one who is *humble and of a contrite spirit.*"[10] David had no trouble recognizing that his own misdeeds resulted from poor choices and sinful desires. Yet, the Father loved him because David's heart remained malleable to His Spirit.

David articulated his dependence upon the Father's protection in Psalm 28:7 when he said, "The Lord is my strength and my shield; My heart trusted in Him and I am helped; Therefore, my heart greatly rejoices, and with my song I will praise Him." The word "shield" (*magen*) communicates empowerment as well as protection. Recognizing God's sovereignty, the heart of the psalmist trusts, whereas the hearts of the wicked were filled with mischief (*ra a*).[11] Additionally, the Psalmist declares, "With my whole heart I have sought you; Oh let me not wander from your commandments. Your word I have hidden in my heart, that I might not sin against you" (Ps. 119:10-11). "Verse 11 is reminiscent of Jer. 31:33, a verse in which God promises to

[9] Walter J. Harrelson et al., *The New Interpreter's Bible: General Articles & Introduction, Commentary, & Reflections for Each Book of the Bible, Including the Apocryphal/Deuterocanonical Books* (Nashville: Abingdon Press, 1994), 88.
[10] John D. W Watts, *Isaiah. 34-66* (Waco: Word Books, 1987), 364.
[11] Harrelson, 789.

write 'instruction' on the people's hearts. In short, God will teach the people directly (Jer. 31:34), a conviction also evident in Ps. 119:12 and throughout the psalm."[12] The passage implies two things: God has more to reveal and the psalmist has more to learn.

The psalmist reiterates the compelling benefits of being in close proximity to the Father's heart. "I know that the Lord will maintain the cause of the afflicted, and justice for the poor. Surely the righteous shall give thanks to your name; the upright shall dwell in your presence," (Ps. 140:12-13). George Angus Fulton Knight emphasizes, "As we have seen in other Psalms, here is a form of speech used in a profession of faith. So he is declaring: *I know that the Lord* cares for the one who suffers this violence and this slander. We should remember that this psalm was written for all ages of man, so that it now includes 'me!'"[13] The transcendence of God's plan for humankind reveals the absolute faithfulness of a God who not only desires the fellowship of His creation, but also offers justice and protection for those who cannot defend themselves.

Then a very strong exclamation follows: *Surely the righteous,* the members of God's Covenant people, will always give thanks that that is what God is like (and not like the Greek gods whom the Israelites were now learning about, and who were always ready to hurl thunderbolts!), so that, as *the upright,* they will continue to *dwell in His presence.* And they shall not do so, come what may, slandered or not, whether they are sufferers from violence or not; for whatever happens in the world, nothing can make any difference to those who

---

12 Ibid., 1169.
13 George Angus Fulton Knight, *Psalms*, Daily Study Bible—Old Testament (Philadelphia: Westminster Press, 1982), 329.

*dwell in His presence.*[14]

The upright knows both the joy and benefit from having been in the presence of the Father. They understand that nothing else can prepare them for life's rigors or produce the quality of fellowship and life necessary to please Him. After David fled from Saul and hid in a cave, he wrote, "My heart is steadfast, O God, my heart is steadfast," (Ps. 57:7). David knew that God knew his heart and that he could trust Him for whatever chain of events unfolded in his life. He rightly avows, "Teach me your way, O Lord; I will walk in Your truth" (86:11). "The word 'truth' (*emet*) in v. 11 is the same as "faithfulness" in v. 15. The psalmist desires life and identity to be shaped by God's will and God's way. In other words, the psalmist gladly submits to God's sovereign rule."[15]

---

*Intentional leaders regularly seek the presence of the Father and deliberately make the search a part of their quests for self-leadership and personal spiritual formation.*

---

Moses led what history considers an incredible emancipation. He realized that without the presence of God to guide his people, the wilderness wandering promised to continue. He poignantly revealed the sentiment of a heart that knew the overwhelming presence and needed the continued guidance of the Father. Then he said to Him, "If Your presence does not go with us, do not bring us up from here. For how will it then be known that Your people and I have found grace in Your sight, except You go with us? So shall we be separate, Your people and I, from all the people who are

---

[14] Ibid., 330.
[15] Harrelson, 1021.

on the face of the earth." Then the Lord said to Moses, "I will also do this thing that you have spoken; for you have found grace in my sight, and I know you by name," (Exod. 33:15-17).

God knew him by name because Moses obediently executed the directives He gave him to accomplish. "Moses' close relationship with God started at the burning bush, and he kept close to that flame his whole life."[16] He diligently sought God's counsel in dealing with a mass of transplanted humanity and endured a generation of having to deal with people who had trouble assimilating the miraculous works God performed among them.

Scriptural narratives abound with the importance of God's servants finding and maintaining a close proximity to His heart. After his encounter with the wicked queen Jezebel, Elijah escaped into the wilderness, lapsed into a state of self-pity, and desired to die. During a pensive moment in a cave, God spoke to him and asked, "What are you doing here, Elijah?" (1 Kings 19:9). Elijah began the litany about his own faithfulness and how he alone remained. He assumed that all the prophets died at Jezebel's bequest and that Israel's spiritual climate changed to accommodate her Phoenician god of fertility, Baal, and the Canaanite goddess of fertility, Asherah.[17] He had no knowledge of Obadiah's preventative protection in which he hid one hundred prophets, fifty each in two different caves (18:4). Elijah's assumption of sole survivorship of Jezebel's purge drove him to the remote cave in which God confronted him and restored a spirit of

---

[16] Hans Finzel, *The Top Ten Leadership Commandments* (Colorado Springs: David C. Cook, 2012), 169.
[17] S. Michael Houdmann, "Who was Asherah/Ashtoreth?" GotQuestions.org, http://www.gotquestions.org/who-Asherah.html (accessed July 21, 2013).

optimism in the prophet's heart.

God demonstrated to Elijah that his incomplete perspective drove him to a place far from the heart of the Father. He told Elijah to "Go out, and stand on the mountain before the Lord," (1 Kings 18:11). As he complied with God's directive, a great wind arose and tore into the mountain, destroying even the rocks, "but the Lord was not in the wind," (v.11). An earthquake followed the wind, "but the Lord was not in the earthquake." A great fire followed the earthquake, "but the Lord was not in the fire," (v. 12). Then, after the demonstrative effects of the wind, earthquake and fire came, "a still small voice," (v. 12). Elijah heard the voice. Hearing it required proximity to the heart of the Father, not the powerful display of nature's dynamics. The narrative reveals the subsequent actions of anointing Jehu as king in Israel and calling Elisha to be his eventual replacement (v. 16). Obedience required Elijah to rediscover authentic communication with the Father. Elijah allowed the pressures and dynamics of the society for which he spoke God's decrees to dictate his physical course of action. Balance to his spiritual perspective returned when he again heard the "still small voice" (v. 12) and regained the necessary proximity to the heart of the Father.

The prophet Isaiah exhorted, "Seek the Lord while He may be found, call upon Him while He is near," (55:6). Augustine queried, "How then am I to seek for you, Lord? Is not the happy life that which I desire, which indeed no one fails to desire?"[18] Intentional leaders regularly seek the presence of the Father and deliberately make the search a part of their quests for self-leadership and personal spiritual

[18] Augustine, *Confessions*, The World's Classics (Oxford: Oxford University Press, 1992), 196.

formation.

"Draw near to God in humility, by walking in his footsteps, and he will draw near to you in his mercy, setting you free from all anxiety. For nobody is far away from God in terms of physical distance; the problem is one of attitudes and emotions. For the person who is anxious to do what is right is always near to God, whereas the one who is lost in his wickedness is far away from him, regardless of where either one happens to live."[19]

The intentionality of "drawing near to God," characterizes the leader's pursuit to *gain close proximity to the heart of the Father.* Until the leader finds that place, no other efforts to please God can suffice. Since God knows the heart of humankind, He knows the thoughts and intent of each individual and whether gaining His presence really constitutes a priority to them.

---

*What a person does in private determines what he or she becomes in public.*

---

Effective leadership emancipates change in others while affecting the personal change necessary to arrive at one's divinely ordained destination in life. This book argues the need for personal change and discusses the trajectory a leader's life should take toward becoming a leader who understands one's personal mission mandate and the process involved in its accomplishment. The imprint of a leader's life produces either fodder for ridicule or an example worthy of replication. Author Gene Wilkes avows, "If all you have to offer are words, few people will follow you. Your example

---

[19] *Patrologia Latina Database*, CD-ROM ed (Alexandria, VA: Chadwyck-Healey, 1995), 93:34.

will give them a picture of what you are talking about."[20] The essential nature of personal discipline demands leadership by example, not only theory. If a spiritual leader has not incorporated the regular exercise of the disciplines associated with finding God's will, his or her leadership cannot survive the rigors demanded in facilitating change nor can it rightly interpret leadership's imperative to guide others toward the personal change that leadership effectiveness requires.

Spiritual formation is the ongoing process of the triune God transforming the believer's life and character toward the life and character of Jesus Christ—accomplished by the ministry of the Spirit in the context of biblical community.[21] Dallas Willard stresses, "The Holy Spirit and other spiritual agencies may think of spiritual formation as a shaping by the Spirit or by the spiritual realm, and involved in the kingdom of God, especially the Word of God. We speak of spiritual formation here because the means (or agencies) that do the shaping of the human personality and life are spiritual."[22]

The content of this chapter aligns with spiritual formation in Christ—not spiritual formation in a generic and general sense as postulated by current cultural paradigms. Willard also believes that, "spirituality is the arena in which specifically Christian faith and practice will have to struggle to retain integrity. Additionally, much of the current distress on the part of Western Christianity over how to conduct our

[20] Gene Wilkes, *Jesus on Leadership* (Wheaton: Tyndale House, 1998), 171.

[21] Paul Pettit, ed., *Foundations of Spiritual Formation: Community Approach to Becoming Like Christ* (Grand Rapids: Kregel Publications, 2008), 24.

[22] Dallas Willard, "Spiritual Formation In Christ: A Perspective On What It Is And How It Might Be Done," *Journal Of Psychology And Theology* 28 (2000): 2.

calling as the people of Christ derives from the fact that the goal and measure of Christian spiritual formation, as described previously, is not accepted and implemented."[23]

A need to be both culturally relevant and biblically sound drives the present quest for understanding of spiritual formation. The need for balance, both in the assessment of the initial information gathering and in the subsequent implementation of that information, provides a metric wherein the process may be fairly evaluated.

---

*Authentic leadership derives valuable insight and spiritual intuition gained only from a relationship in which a loving Father imparts first-hand instruction to a heart capable of hearing Him.*

---

In his book, *The Continuing Conversion of the Church*, Derrell Guder emphatically asserts that Western Christian influence has reduced the gospel to something it can manage rather than allowing God to work without ecclesiastical restrictions or boundaries.[24] The plight of Christian spiritual formation charts a course through (though not inclusive of) the reduced expression of Western Christianity to arrive at the destination revealed only through the development and exercise of personal spiritual disciplines. What a person does in private determines what he or she becomes in public. "The discontinuity between a leader's private life and his public leadership has become rather alarming to those concerned with integrity and character. The argument is based on the faulty premise that a leader's deeply held values and beliefs are not consequential or in any way causative when it comes

---

[23] Ibid.

[24] Darrell L. Guder, *The Continuing Conversion of the Church* (Grand Rapids: W. B. Eerdmans, 2000), locations 1576–1601.

to his public behavior and the manner in which he exercises his leadership on the public stage."[25]

Effective leadership emanates from a heart that has found its way into the transforming presence of the Father. Transformative leadership dare not hinge on experience or knowledge alone, but on the daily renewing of one's thoughts, strengths, and convictions. Competent and confident leadership produces clarity of mission and seeks to accurately interpret directives from the Father's heart. Personal leadership that has not been transformed by the Father gravitates to the lowest common denominator in which techniques and methods trump the "new thing" God desires to accomplish within the heart of a leader and within a people called by His name (Isa. 43:19). Mission becomes the template into which the leader must fit as the retooling of ministry gifts and reframing of ministry context takes precedence over conventionality and familiar methodology.

Authentic leadership derives valuable insight and spiritual intuition gained only from a relationship in which a loving Father imparts first-hand instruction to a heart capable of hearing Him. Anything else cannot convey the Father's intent to help the leader maximize his or her gifts nor can it produce the discernment necessary to lead. Having studied the leadership style and personal spirituality of Charles Spurgeon, Samuel Rima relates, "Spurgeon rightly recognized that the ultimate success of a leader will be determined by how well [he or] she masters the inner life."[26] Since God sees the heart of an individual, He knows the composition of a leader's true spirituality and the authenticity of their commitment to Him. "… and your Father who sees in secret

---

[25] Rima, 25.
[26] Ibid., 14.

will himself reward you openly" (Matt. 6:4). It is of paramount importance that the leader develop a private walk with God in which he or she learns to navigate through the myriad of decisions they will be called upon to make.

Time alone with the Father reveals things that reading books and attending seminars will not. Leadership born of revelation is leadership with substance. Conversely, leadership lacking fresh revelation is destined to wither on the vine like a plant without water. Earl Creps points out that virtually every influential leader he has known has emerged from a crisis of personal transformation in which they experience a paradigm crash that changes their orientation toward ministry. "Sometimes violent, sometimes gradual, paradigm crashes create an opportunity for God to take me off road, awakening me to mission by crucifying aspects of my culture, leadership, and spirituality that, unbeknownst to me, need to die."[27] Effective ministry flows from the Father's heart. Without input from *proximity to the Father's heart*, one cannot really know His will and therefore cannot really implement it within the context of ministry. The gospel gets reduced to a manageable set of guidelines, and real transformation gets lost.

An alarming rate of dropout among pastors and spiritual leaders fuels the need for a personal inventory of spiritual disciplines. According to a 2006 survey conducted by Richard Krejcir, of the 1,050 pastors surveyed, every one had a close associate or seminary friend who had left the ministry because of burnout, church conflict, or from a moral failure.[28]

[27] Earl G. Creps, *Off-road Disciplines: Spiritual Adventures of Missional Leaders* (San Francisco: Jossey-Bass, 2006), 4.

[28] Richard J. Krejcir, "What Is Going On With the Pastors in America?" Into Thy Word,

Additionally, Krejcir reveals,

- Nine hundred forty-eight (948 or 90%) of pastors stated they are frequently fatigued, and worn out on a weekly and even daily basis (did not say *burned out*).
- Nine hundred thirty-five, (935 or 89%) of the pastors we surveyed also considered leaving the ministry at one time. Five hundred ninety, (590 or 57%) said they would leave if they had a better place to go-including secular work.
- Eighty-one percent (81%) of the pastors said there was no regular discipleship program or effective effort of mentoring their people or teaching them to deepen their Christian formation at their church.
- Eight hundred eight (808 or 77%) of the pastors we surveyed felt they did not have a good marriage!
- Seven hundred ninety (790 or 75%) of the pastors we surveyed felt they were unqualified and/or poorly trained by their seminaries to lead and manage the church or to counsel others. This left them disheartened in their ability to pastor.
- Seven hundred fifty-six (756 or 72%) of the pastors we surveyed stated that they only studied the Bible when they were preparing for sermons or lessons. This left only 28% who read the Bible for devotions and personal study.
- Eight hundred two (802 or 71%) of pastors stated they were burned out, and they battle depression beyond fatigue on a weekly and even a daily basis.

---

Http://www.intothyword.org/apps/articles/?articleid=36562 (accessed April 15, 2013).

- Three hundred ninety-nine (399 or 38%) of pastors said they were divorced or currently in a divorce process.
- Three hundred fifteen (315 or 30%) said they had either been in an ongoing affair or a one-time sexual encounter with a parishioner
- Two hundred seventy (270 or 26%) of pastors said they regularly had personal devotions and felt they were adequately fed spiritually.
- Two hundred forty-one (241 or 23%) of the pastors we surveyed said they felt happy and content on a regular basis with who they are in Christ, in their church, and in their home!
- Of the pastors surveyed, they stated that a mean (average) of only 25% of their church's membership attended a Bible Study or small group at least twice a month.[29]

While a professor of leadership at Fuller Theological Seminary, Bobby Clinton did a comparative study of leadership in the Scriptures. Of the approximately one thousand leaders mentioned by name in the Bible, only 30 percent finished strong. Current comparable leadership statistics reveal a shocking similarity—30 percent finish well.[30]

Statistics reveal the apparent foundational collapse in the lives and ministries of people who responded to God's call into ministry but failed to establish a personal template of spiritual formation. They failed to lead their churches effectively because they omitted the personal disciplines

---

[29] Ibid.
[30] Richard Clinton and Paul Leavenworth, *Starting Well* (Des Moines: Convergence Publishing, 2012), 4.

necessary to maintain a healthy growth trajectory. The resultant dropout and failure rates provide impetus for the establishment of and adherence to a set of vital components designed to provide balance and traction in a leader's personal development.

> *The realization that God desires believers to engage their culture in His strength produces confidence in a resource that lacks nothing.*

The discipline of Proximity governs the activities produced by Solitude, Sabbatical, Solidarity, and Strategy. All four components *require* proximity to the heart of the Father. Everything believers do must be gauged by a proper relationship with the Author of life. Christians often ask God to bless their plans and activities without ever asking Him for *His* plan. They do not think of joining Him but rather ask Him to join them in their endeavor and bless whatever they do in ministry. When "we pass from thinking of God as part of our life (compartmentalization) to the realization that we are part of his life. … a conversion of the heart takes place."[31] Alan Hirsch maintains that, "Christology must define all that we do and say. It means that in order to recover the ethos of authentic Christianity, we need to refocus our attention back to the Root of it all, to recalibrate ourselves and our organizations around the person and work of Jesus the Lord."[32]

The realization that God desires believers to engage their culture in His strength produces confidence in a resource that

---

[31] Richard J. Foster, *Prayer: Finding the Heart's True Home* (New York: HarperCollins Publishers 1992), 15.

[32] Alan Hirsch, *The Forgotten Ways: Reactivating the Missional Church* (Grand Rapids: Brazos Press, 2006), 94.

lacks nothing. Leaders must understand what needs to take place both in transformational thinking and belief. God desires to bring order and success to their otherwise cluttered effort to please Him and leave their mark on the ministry to which He called them. They must be aligned with His greater purpose and begin to function in the perspective of surrender to that purpose. He must be at the center of everything they value and everything they seek to do in His name. Attempts at productivity take on new life as leaders segue from their former mode of self-empowerment to God-empowerment and begin to enjoy His reserve of strength and fortitude.

King David and three of his mighty men sat in the cave at Adullam and allowed their deepest longings to surface. David recounted the taste of the water from the well near the gate in Bethlehem and said, "Oh, that someone would give me a drink of water from the well of Bethlehem, which is by the gate!" (1 Chron. 11:15-19). Though he did not intend for his men to break through the Philistine guard and bring him a drink of that special water, his wish became their command. They heard his heart and willingly risked their lives for him. Their close physical proximity gauged their actions and fueled their response. They wanted only to please their master.

Leaders cannot hear from the Father if they do not remain near enough to hear the content of His heart. The Proximity Factor determines the state of the whole model of personal spirituality and must characterize the leader's intent to proceed only after hearing from the Father. This book attempts to articulate the value and necessity of proximity to the Father's heart and discusses the four components of Solitude, Sabbatical, Solidarity, and Strategy in relationship to the leader's personal spiritual formation.

*Leaders cannot hear from the Father if they do not
remain near enough to hear the content of His heart.*

The disciplines of Solitude, Sabbatical, and Solidarity must be in Proximity to the Father's heart so that Strategy for life and ministry may emerge with confidence and intentionality in the leader. The disciplines must guide the leader's trajectory through the opportunities in which that leader applies his or her influence as a mentor and leader.

# CHAPTER 4

# Solitude: Staying Sensitive

*Personal times of solitude demand willingness to allow the "still small voice" of the Father to permeate one's innermost being and reveal His compassionate care and providential plan for each leader.*

Solitude refers to time spent alone with God and receives the protection of top priority. He does not need to compete with external activities or demands. Personal times of solitude demand willingness to allow the "still small voice" of the Father to permeate one's innermost being and reveal His compassionate care and providential plan for each leader. "Leaders in ministry cannot succeed in the realms of the spirit without the 'God factor.' Our relationship with Him affects every aspect of our leadership. Time spent with Him translates into power for His cause."[33] Philip Hughes adds,

---

[33] Hans Finzel, *The Top Ten Leadership Commandments* (Colorado Springs: David C. Cook, 2012), 165.

"The doctrine of man (anthropology) can be truly apprehended only in the light of the doctrine of Christ (Christology). Not only the destiny but also the origin of man involves a profound relationship with the Second Person of the Holy Trinity. Indeed, mankind's origin in Christ ... Man's destiny, implicit in his origin, is the attainment of the "complete knowledge of the Son of God" which coincides with his becoming "the perfect man," his arrival at "the measure of the stature of the fullness of Christ" (Eph. 4:13). Christ, accordingly, is the True Image in which man was formed at creation and into which by the reconciling grace of re-creation fallen man is being transformed.[34]

Spiritual formation cannot exist without the partnership between God the Father and humankind. Hughes asserts that the second person of the Holy Trinity provides humanity with its destiny and that destiny cannot exist without the resourceful partnership of God the Father. The two must go together. Solitude provides the opportunity to dwell in the presence of the Father and simply to listen as He imparts vital components of understanding and revelation. Mays emphasizes, "instruction comes from God, but it must become a part of the servant of God. It must be gathered into the store of the heart, the mind and mentality with which one thinks and wills."[35] Ester Buchholz, in an article written for *Psychology Today* taken from her book, "The Call of Solitude," acknowledges, "For religion to have its greatest

---

[34] Philip Edgcumbe Hughes, *The True Image: The Origin and Destiny of Man in Christ* (Grand Rapids: Eerdmans, 1989), viii–ix.

[35] James Luther Mays, *Psalms*, Interpretation (Louisville: John Knox Press, 1994), 385.

appeal, it must allow time for solitude."[36] She adds, "Religion must provide time for prayer and meditation. And the relationship of the individual to God is one solution to the paradox of aloneness and relatedness."[37] The secular academic community recognizes the importance of the discipline of solitude in one form or another. Buchholz hints at the connection between humankind's need and God's awareness of it. "The goal of solitude centers on gaining sensitivity in a human heart capable of deceit and self-sufficiency. Richard Foster stresses that the fruit of solitude manifests itself in "increased sensitivity and compassion for others and a new freedom to be with people."[38]

Solitude filters out the mundane mindsets that characterize daily dealings and provide significance to our perspectives. St. John of the Cross indicates that during times of solitude when he had to walk in darkness, a gracious protection from vices and a wonderful advance in the things of the Father's kingdom came into clear focus. He states, "A person at the time of these darknesses ... will see clearly how little the appetites and faculties are distracted with useless and harmful things and how secure he is from vainglory, from pride and presumption, from an empty and false joy, and from many other evils."[39] Additionally, solitude "permits you to retreat from the press and struggle in order to let your

---

[36] Ester Buchholz, "The Call of Solitude," *Psychology Today,* January 2012, http://www.psychologytoday.com/articles/199802/the-call-solitude (accessed September 3, 2013).

[37] Ibid.

[38] Richard J. Foster, *Celebration of Discipline: The Path to Spiritual Growth,* rev. 1st ed. (San Francisco: Harper & Row, 1988), 108.

[39] John of the Cross, *The Collected Works of Saint John of the Cross,* rev. ed (Washington: ICS Publications, 1991), 364.

fragmented and dispersed self become collected."[40] Humankind's inability to self direct in spiritual matters drives the need for regular times of solitude wherein the Father directs His will to the cognizance of the seeker. Dallas Willard stresses, "There is a place for effort, but it must never take God's place with us. We need to make room for him in our lives."[41]

---

*Solitude filters out the mundane mindsets that characterize daily dealings and provide significance to our perspectives.*

---

Solitude requires the temporary abandonment of everything capable of competing with the voice of God. The word "solitude" evokes mental images of aloneness and isolation. While the leader's life tends to be lonely due to the isolation that comes from carrying too much of the burden alone and, "not having a safe place for one's own soul,"[42] leaders still need to find a place and time in which they can experience the refortifying of their inner fortress and a refilling of their inner reservoir. Time spent alone with God produces a heightened sense of spiritual sensitivity necessary for navigating the rigors of leadership and gaining trust in an unfailing Father who knows the human heart. That trust "guides the immediate refashioning of our being, the

---

[40] E. Glenn Hinson, *Spiritual Preparation for Christian Leadership* (Nashville: Upper Room Books, 1999), 55.

[41] Dallas Willard, "Let Christ Do the Real Work," *Leadership Journal*, no.2 (Fall 2011), under "Where I Find Refreshment," http://www.christianitytoday.com/le/2011/fall/findrefreshment.html (accessed September 3, 2013).

[42] Ruth Haley Barton, *Strengthening the Soul of Your Leadership: Seeking God in the Crucible of Ministry* (Downers Grove, IL: IVP Books, 2008), 169.

transformation of our pain, woundedness, and unconscious motivation into the person that God intended us to be."[43] Only time spent in secret with God produces the depth of relationship capable of offering to others what is gained in private. During time alone with Him leaders gain insight into His plan and foresight for the next steps. "It is impossible to overstate how dangerous we can become as leaders if we are not routinely inviting God to search us and know us and lead us in a new way."[44] A leader cannot compete with the barrage of worldly content if he or she has not met with God and been truly alone with Him. Within those quiet times when the voice of God seeks audience with the leader's spirit, He seeks to build in them the character necessary for the tests to come. Solitude permits leaders to "retreat from the press and struggle in order to let their fragmented and dispersed self become collected."[45] Leonard Sweet adds clarification to the eventual product of solitude. "What matters is not the products you make, but the virtues that make you."[46] Leaders who make the intentional effort to gain the Father's presence come away satisfied and determined to come again. The Father's intent is to simply speak to every listening heart and fill it with His power for living.

The value of solitude cannot be measured without the goal of knowing God better and learning to trust His plan as implemented through one's leadership. J. I. Packer posits,

---

[43] Thomas Keating, *Intimacy with God* (New York: Crossroad, 1994), 22.

[44] Barton, 127.

[45] E. Glenn Hinson, *Spiritual Preparation for Christian Leadership* (Nashville: Upper Room Books, 1999), 55.

[46] Leonard Sweet, *Summoned to Lead* (Grand Rapids: Zondervan, 2004), 38.

"We must say that knowing God involves, first, listening to God's word and receiving it as the Holy Spirit interprets it, in application to oneself; second, noting God's nature and character, as His word and works reveal it; third, accepting His invitations, and doing what He commands; fourth, recognizing, and rejoicing in, the love that He has shown in thus approaching one and drawing one into this divine fellowship."[47]

The physical venue for solitude is not as important as the spiritual intentionality that mandates a deliberate time set aside for daily space alone with God. "Leaders in ministry cannot succeed in the realms of the spirit without the 'God factor.' Our relationship with Him affects every aspect of our leadership. Time spent with Him translates into power for His cause."[48]

While Richard Foster views solitude as a state of mind and heart rather than a place,[49] the selection of a time and place for individual solitude with the Father drastically improves the likelihood of the discipline taking root in the leader's life. Some assume that "highway time" provides the opportunity to be away from the phone and other distractions germane to one's vocation or ministry. While the driver can control things such as phones and music, they must still pay attention to other traffic. So, in truth, the Father does not have his or her full attention. Even though some leaders espouse their ability to experience solitude while driving, they must still be aware of the external world through

---

[47] J. I. Packer, *Knowing God* (Downers Grove, IL: InterVarsity Press, 1973), 32.

[48] Hans Finzel, *The Top Ten Leadership Commandments* (Colorado Springs: David C. Cook, 2012), 165.

[49] Richard J. Foster, *Celebration of Discipline: The Path to Spiritual Growth*, rev. 1st ed. (San Francisco: Harper & Row, 1988), 96.

which they must pass and the potential "calls to attention" intrinsic to traveling a public roadway. Those times can be considered "quiet time" but not solitude.

Solitude adheres to the discipline of Proximity and satisfies four questions. First, the leader must assume proximity to the heart of God. Position requires an awareness of the leader's physical venue and what he or she can do to be alone with God and to experience His acceptance and guidance. The leader will only be able to demonstrate acceptance of others if he or she has experienced the discernible acceptance of God. The experience of God's acceptance "frees us from our needy self and thus creates new space where we can pay selfless attention to others."[50] Whether an early morning walk before the world awakens or sitting in a favorite chair before the sun comes up, the leader must deliberately place him or herself in a position free of expectations, demands, and distractions. "Learning to pay attention and knowing what to pay attention to is a key discipline for leaders but one that rarely comes naturally to those of us who are barreling through life with our eyes fixed on a goal."[51] Solitude provides a clutter-free environment in which the spirit may hear and receive instructions from a Father jealous for the leader's time and attention.

---

*Only solitude provides the opportunity for the Father to speak to a receptive heart and to illumine darkness resident there.*

---

Second, the purpose of the leader's time in solitude cannot be to convince God to bless his or her plans, but

---

[50] Henri J. Nouwen, *The Selfless Way of Christ: Downward Mobility and the Spiritual Life* (Maryknoll, NY: Orbis Books, 2007), 58.

[51] Barton, 63.

rather to proceed only after hearing His voice. Solitude can produce an atmosphere in which leaders can discern the voice of God from the myriads of voices competing for their attention. Saint John of the Cross poignantly notes, "My house being all now stilled."[52] The silent and still time in which the leader gains the presence of the Father and discerns His heart guides decision-making and personal growth. Solitude, without a listening heart, holds no prospect of spiritual formation if the leader refuses to allow God to look deep into his or her heart and make needed adjustments. Only solitude provides the opportunity for the Father to speak to a receptive heart and to illumine darkness resident there. There are times when we do the talking and there are times when God does the talking. I call those times Tabernacle times and Garden times. It is in the Tabernacle that we invite God into our presence and WE do the talking—through our praise and worship. During those times, He enjoys listening to His children worshiping and adoring Him. Then, there are Garden times. During those times, He invites us into His presence and HE does the talking and we do the listening. We quiet our hearts and gain the benefits of His love and devotion to us—His loving and deliberate creation.

Third, process involves a deliberate step to gain a solitary place with God. Process implies action. The quest of leadership must be intentional if it is to endure the process associated with gaining additional spiritual insight and sensitivity. Leaders can take no greater action than when they deliberately set a time to gain the presence of God and go

---

[52] John of the Cross, *The Collected Works of Saint John of the Cross*, rev. ed. (Washington, D.C.: ICS Publications, 1991), 296.

there regularly. Foster rightly asserts, "We bore down deeper and deeper, the way a drill would bore down into the bowels of the earth. We are constantly turning inward. It is not a journey *into* ourselves that we are undertaking but a journey *through* ourselves so that we can emerge from the deepest level of the self into God."[53] As the leader gains proximity to the Father's heart, he or she can discern the Father's will in a matter and discover that solitude with Him produces clarity of thinking and objectivity of intent.

---

*Leaders can take no greater action than when they deliberately set a time to gain the presence of God and go there regularly*

---

Since process always demands change, most leaders find the step the most difficult to consistently implement in their daily regimen. Foster avows that the will has the same deficiency as the law—it can deal only with externals. It proves incapable of bringing about the necessary transformation of the inner spirit.[54] Times of solitude produce results that God can only accomplish when He has the undivided attention of the one seeking His presence. "When in honesty we accept the evil that is in us as part of the truth about ourselves and offer that truth up to God, we are in a mysterious way nourished. Even the truth about our shadow side sets us free."[55] The process emotes pain associated with self-will and contrary hearts and reveals hidden agendas and misplaced priorities. The process stage of

---

[53] Foster, *Celebration of Discipline*, 32.

[54] Ibid., 6.
[55] Richard J. Foster, *Prayer: Finding the Heart's True Home* (San Francisco: HarperSanFrancisco, 1992), 31.

spiritual formation drives some leaders closer to the Father's heart while providing an off-ramp for others.

The process also includes regular prayer (remember the Tabernacle times and the Garden times). Solitude without these purposeful spiritual disciplines gains no traction nor produces any appreciable results. The Apostle Paul qualified his personal spiritual formation and the effectiveness with which he lived: "I pray with the spirit, and I will pray with the understanding. I will sing with the spirit and I will sing with the understanding" (1 Cor. 14:15). Prayer reveals God's character of unconditional love for His creation and those He fashioned in His image. "Through a disciplined life of contemplative prayer we slowly can come to realize God's original love, the love that existed long before we could love ourselves or receive any other human love."[56] Communication with God from both spirit and mind continually reinforces confidence in a God who never fails.

Prayer consists more of listening than petitioning. Prayer in solitude provides an opportunity for the leader to allow God to touch his or her life in a personal way. This time of prayer does not focus on intercession and petition. God's self-revelation to the leader is its only goal. From this time of prayer comes the strategy necessary for effectiveness in ministry and living. Walter Wright recounts that his most effective times alone with God come as a result of his listening without distraction—whether praying alone in his room or walking a mountain pathway.[57] The investment of that time acts as a guiding beacon of confidence in God's big

---

[56] Nouwen, 59.

[57] Walter C. Wright, *Relational Leadership: A Biblical Model for Influence and Service* (Carlisle: Paternoster, 2000), 8.

picture over and against his limited human perspective. Placing one's self in the proper position, having a viable purpose, and understanding the process always produces a product. Barton reiterates the priority that must precede the leader's process toward genuine transformation and its intended application. "Our leadership cannot be a force for good if it is not being refined by the rigors of true solitude, that place where God is at work beyond what we are able to do for ourselves or would even know how to do for ourselves."[58] A personal model of spirituality must accurately represent the itinerary designed not only to take leaders into the presence of the Father, but also into that of their enemies. More than half a century ago Thomas Merton commented, "It is in deep solitude that I find the gentleness with which I can truly love my brothers. The more solitary I am the more affection I have for them ... solitude and silence teach me to love my brothers for what they are, not for what they say."[59] Likewise, Foster admits gaining a greater sensitivity to the needs of others.[60]

---

*The process emotes pain associated with self-will and contrary hearts and reveals hidden agendas and misplaced priorities.*

---

Life's ongoing demands have a way of dulling the leader's ability to discern God's voice from the deafening pitch of other voices whose intent aims to distract, delay, and detour the leader from acting on insight and perspective

---

[58] Barton, 43.

[59] Thomas Merton, *The Sign of Jonas*, 1st ed. (New York: Harcourt, Brace, 1953), 261.

[60] Foster, *Celebration of Discipline*, 108.

potentially gained in the Father's presence.

Influence emerges as a discernible by-product of solitude in proximity to the Father's heart. "Influence is about the hidden forces that make visible results that have an enduring effect."[61] Influence becomes apparent in the life of the leader who maintains the essential closeness to God's heart. "Spiritual influence and leadership take place at the level of the human spirit, and they are prompted by the Spirit of God, who works to reform the human spirit, bringing people back to the shape God designed in the first place. Influence happens by the inflow—the in-fluence—of the Spirit. It happens through a thousand hidden, imperceptible steps. It is founded on a real connection with God."[62]

While Psalms 27:5 and 31:20 decry the plots of humanity and the need for God to protect them from errant actions, the essence of authentic solitude draws close to the heart of the Father—whether one is in trouble or not. Psalm 86:11 reveals the true intent of the psalmist as he or she confidently petitions, "Teach me your way, O Lord; I will walk in your truth; Unite my heart to fear your name." The prayer seeks not only deliverance from trouble but also help in the formation of the self. "Unite my heart" is a petition that reaches out for the salvation promised by Jeremiah to the redeemed Israel: "I will give them one heart and one way" (Jer. 32:39).[63] The benefits of proximity to the Father's heart contain more than a desire for personal protection or position. They usher the diligent individual into the awesome presence of a Father who fails not nor wavers at His

---

[61] Mel Lawrenz, *Spiritual Influence: The Hidden Power Behind Leadership* (Grand Rapids: Zondervan, 2012), 27.

[62] Ibid., 30.

[63] Mays, 280.

promises. "Solitude is where spiritual ministry begins. That's where Jesus listened to God. That's where we listen to God."[64] Ruth Haley Barton augments this thought: "The longing for solitude is the longing for God. It is the longing to experience union with God unmediated by the ways we typically try to relate to God. It is the practice that spiritual seekers down through the ages have used to experience intimacy with God rather than just talking about it. Solitude is a place in time that is set apart for God and God alone, a time when we unplug and withdraw from the noise of interpersonal interactions, from the noise, business and constant stimulation associated with life in the company of others."[65] True solitude provides both the discipline of a heart to become quieted and the opportunity for God to speak to a willing individual intent on hearing His plan for their life.

The psalmist uses the word "refuge" in Psalm 91:2 ("and I will say of the Lord, He is my refuge and my fortress") as a metaphor for God's care and protection.[66] The verse emotes classic status on the "sure providence of God as the citadel of faith."[67] Protection comes from confidence in a God who cannot be defeated by an enemy. Alignment with His purpose and plan provide the necessary strategy for effective life and ministry. The psalmist rests in his conviction that God may be found and His counsel obtained when he stated, "I call to

---

[64] Henri Nouwen, "Moving From Solitude to Community to Ministry," *Leadership Journal* 16, no. 2 (Spring 1995): 83.

[65] Ruth Haley Barton, *Sacred Rhythms: Arranging Our Lives for Transformation* (Downers Grove, IL: IVP, 2006), 32.

[66] "Refuge" is frequently utilized in prayers and confessions of confidence in God in noun form (Ps. 14:6; 46:1; 61:3) and as a verb ("take refuge," e.g., Ps. 2:11; 5:11; 11:1).

[67] Mays, 296.

remembrance my song in the night; I meditate within my heart, and my spirit makes diligent search" (Ps. 77:6).

The word "solitude" evokes an image of aloneness or loneliness. As Jesus' public ministry began to gain traction and momentum, He found it increasingly more important to find a place where He could be alone and seek the counsel of His Father—even though it had been a pattern of his entire life. Following a day in which numerous healings took place during Jesus' public ministry, He "went off to a lonely or deserted spot, a quiet retreat."[68] "Now in the morning, having risen a long while before daylight (*proi ennucha lian*), He went out and departed to a solitary place; and there He prayed" (Mark 1:35). The word *proi* in Mark means the last watch of the night from three to six a.m. *Ennucha lian* means the early part of the watch while it was still a bit dark.[69] "Jesus knew the blessing and power of prayer. 'And there He prayed,' (*kakei proseucheto*). Imperfect tense pictured Jesus as praying through the early morning hours."[70] Mark's word "solitary" (*epnous*) also means "desert or barren place."[71] Hendriksen adds, "Jesus attached great importance to prayer. He himself prayed when he was baptized (Lk. 3:21); just before choosing the twelve disciples (Lk. 6:12); in connection with, and after the miraculous feeding of the five thousand (Mk. 6:41, 46; cf. Matt. 14:19, 23); when He was about to ask his disciples an

---

[68] William Hendriksen, *New Testament Commentary* (Grand Rapids: Baker Book House, 1953), 71.

[69] A. T. Robertson, *Word Pictures in the New Testament* (New York: R. R. Smith, 1930), 263.

[70] Ibid., 264.

[71] E. W. Bullinger, *A Critical Lexicon and Concordance to the English and Greek New Testament, Together with an Index of Greek Words, and Several Appendices*, 8th ed. (London: Lamp Press, 1957), 196.

important question (Lk. 9:18)."[72]

Effective solitude requires silence. "Without silence there is no solitude. Though silence sometimes involves the absence of speech, it always involves the act of listening."[73] While fully divine, the incarnational presence of the Godhead still took residence in a human form. Being fully human, Jesus found it necessary to find a solitary place in which He could commune with His Father and gain His divine perspective and refresh his heart. Larry Richards explains, "The Hebrew word *leb* is usually found where the NIV and NASB read "heart." It is a broad, inclusive term. In our culture, we tend to divide a human being into isolated functions, such as the spiritual, the intellectual, the emotional, the rational, and the violational. But the Hebrew thought maintains the unity of the person. It looks at a human being as a whole and expresses all of these and other inner human functions by use of the word *leb*."[74]

---

*The transformation of a human's heart demands a time of solitude with which nothing can compete except the overwhelming love of the Father and His desire to impart that love into a receptive heart.*

---

Since Jesus maintained human form, His heart identified with that form. His susceptibility to human physical weaknesses left Him in need of close proximity to His Father's heart. R. A. Cole states, "He (Jesus) was accustomed to spend his 'preacher's Monday morning.' The earliness of the hour and the pains taken to secure a quiet place for

---

[72] Hendriksen, 71.

[73] Foster, 25.

[74] Larry Richards, *Expository Dictionary of Bible Words* (Grand Rapids: Regency Reference Library, 1985), 334.

uninterrupted prayer left a lasting impression on the disciples."[75] Jesus maintained the familiar place with His Father. "And Jesus lifted up His eyes and said, 'Father, I thank You that You have heard Me. And I know that You always hear Me,'" (John 11:41-42). He could make that statement having never been turned away from the intimate fellowship produced by His close proximity to the Father's heart. His practice of solitude produced results for His continued presence in the world, and served as an example for all others to follow.

The psalmist reiterates the compelling benefits of being in close proximity to the Father's heart. "I know that the Lord will maintain the cause of the afflicted, and justice for the poor. Surely the righteous shall give thanks to your name; the upright shall dwell in your presence," (Ps. 140:12-13). "As we have seen in other Psalms, here is a form of speech used in a profession of faith. So he is declaring: *I know that the Lord* cares for the one who suffers this violence and this slander.

We should remember that this psalm was written for all ages of man, so that it now includes 'me!'"[76] The transcendence of God's plan for humankind reveals the absolute faithfulness of a God who not only desires the fellowship of His creation, but also offers justice and protection for those who cannot defend themselves.

Scriptural narratives abound with the importance of God's servants finding and maintaining a close proximity to His heart through the discipline of solitude. After his encounter with the wicked queen Jezebel, Elijah escaped into

---

[75] R. A. Cole, *The Gospel According to Mark: An Introduction and Commentary*, The Tyndale New Testament Commentaries, 2nd ed., rev. ed, (Grand Rapids: IVP, 1989), 117.

[76] George Angus Fulton Knight, *Psalms*, Daily Study Bible—Old Testament (Philadelphia: Westminster Press, 1982), 329.

the wilderness, lapsed into a state of self-pity, and desired to die. During a pensive moment in a cave, God spoke to him and asked, "What are you doing here, Elijah?" (1 Kings 19:9). Elijah began the litany about his own faithfulness and how he alone remained. He assumed that all the prophets died at Jezebel's bequest and that Israel's spiritual climate changed to accommodate her Phoenician god of fertility, Baal, and the Canaanite goddess of fertility, Asherah.[77] He had no knowledge of Obadiah's preventative protection in which he hid one hundred prophets, fifty each in two different caves (18:4). Elijah's assumption of sole survivorship of Jezebel's purge drove him to the remote cave in which God confronted him and restored a spirit of optimism in the prophet's heart.

Jesus valued the time spent alone with His Father. He knew that time had both redemptive and transformative power for effective leadership. Matthew records Jesus' assessment of time spent in solitude with the Father. "For where your treasure is, there your heart will be also" (Matt. 6:21). The thing a person treasures becomes the focus of his or her life and personality. Thomas Merton stresses that solitude and the resultant meditation "has no point and no reality unless it is firmly rooted in life."[78] John R. W. Stott declares, "I believe that those who are not eminently holy pray little and those who are eminently holy pray much. Again, prayer and sinning will never live together in the same

---

[77] S. Michael Houdmann, "Who was Asherah/Ashtoreth?" GotQuestions.org, http://www.gotquestions.org/who-Asherah.html (accessed July 21, 2013).

[78] Thomas Merton, *Contemplative Prayer* (New York: Herder and Herder, 1969), 39.

heart. Prayer will consume sin, or sin will choke prayer."[79] The transformation of a human's heart demands a time of solitude with which nothing can compete except the overwhelming love of the Father and His desire to impart that love into a receptive heart. "Whoever intends to come to an inward fixing of his heart upon God and to have the grace of devotion must with our Savior Christ withdraw from the world."[80]

The leader's determination to separate himself or herself from the rigors of life to a quiet place finds a directive in Matthew 6:6. "But you, when you pray, go into your room, and when you have shut your door, pray to your Father who is in the secret place; and your Father who sees in secret will reward you openly." The import of this passage plainly infers that entering one's personal prayer room should be a personal matter—not a public demonstration of piety. Robertson clarifies, "Into your room" - The word is a late syncopated form of *tambieion* from *tamais* (steward) and the root *tam-* from *temno,* to cut. So it is a storehouse, a separate apartment, one's private chamber, closet, or "den" where he can withdraw from the world and shut the world out and commune with God.[81] The place of solitude must be a place free from interruption and multi-tasking.

Authentic solitude produces a suitable venue and state of mind that evokes a quieting of the human spirit and invites the Spirit of God to communicate His will. The leader discovers the luxury of uninterrupted prayer to the Father who always responds to the inquiring heart. "Prayer catapults

---

[79] John R. W. Stott, *Christian Basics: An Invitation to Discipleship,* 2nd ed. (Grand Rapids: Baker Books, 2003), 118–19.
[80] Thomas and William C. Creasy, eds., *The Imitation of Christ* (Macon: Mercer University Press, 1989), 56.
[81] Robertson, 51.

us onto the frontier of the spiritual life. Meditation introduces us to the inner life, fasting is an accompanying means, study transforms our minds, but prayer brings us into the deepest and highest work of the human spirit."[82] Creasy instructs, "Shut fast the door of your soul—that is to say, your imagination—and keep it cautiously, as much as you can, from beholding any earthly thing."[83] Solitude necessitates the discipline of self-management and self-control if the leader values the prospect of personal spiritual formation consistent with the sovereign plan of the Father. Keating elaborates, "The Christian spiritual path is based on a deepening trust in God. It is trust that first allows us to take that initial leap in the dark, to encounter God at deeper levels of ourselves. And it is trust that guides the immediate refashioning of our being, the transformation of our pain, woundedness, and unconscious motivation into the person that God intended us to be."[84]

---

*Solitude necessitates the discipline of self-management..*

---

The premise of a consciousness open only to the Father produces opportunity for the leader to shut out everything except the "still small voice" of the Spirit of God. Only in silence can he or she place him or herself in the position to hear that voice. "Silence goes hand in hand with solitude. Silence sensitizes, just as noise desensitizes."[85] The Father speaks to the heart that fully focuses its attention upon Him and desperately wants the transformation produced by that

---

82 Foster, 33.
83 Thomas and Creasy, 58.
84 Thomas Keating, *Intimacy with God* (New York: Crossroad, 1994), 22.
85 Hinson, 55.

time together. Solitude produces the opportunity to fully know God's desire for the leader's life. Packer posits, "We must say that knowing God involves, first, listening to God's word and receiving it as the Holy Spirit interprets it, in application to oneself; second, noting God's nature and character, as His word and works reveal it; third, accepting His invitations, and doing what He commands; fourth, recognizing, and rejoicing in, the love that He has shown in thus approaching one and drawing one into this divine fellowship."[86]

The Apostle Paul's second letter to the church at Corinth articulated the product of having been in the presence of the Father. "And we, who are with unveiled faces all reflect the Lord's glory, are being transformed into his likeness with ever-increasing glory, which comes from the Lord, who is the Spirit," (2 Cor. 3:18). Transformation comes only from the One who has the capability to transform.

*A new quality of relationship emerges that replaces the remnants of humanity's carnal nature.*

Solitude produces a meditative mindset in which the leader quiets his or her own heart. "Christian meditation, very simply, is the ability to hear God's voice and obey his word. It involves no hidden mysteries, no secret mantras, no mental gymnastics, no esoteric flights into the cosmic consciousness."[87] It involves only the obedient heart determined to affix itself to the heart of the Father and respond obediently in all it does. A new quality of relationship emerges that replaces the remnants of humanity's

[86] J. I. Packer, *Knowing God* (Downers Grove: InterVarsity Press, 1973), 32.
[87] Foster, 17.

carnal nature. New perspectives take root in once infertile hearts and the love with which the Father loves becomes incarnational in those hearts. Merton reveals, "It is in deep solitude that I find the gentleness with which I can truly love my brothers. The more solitary I am the more affection I have for them … solitude and silence teach me to love my brothers for what they are, not for what they say."[88] The wise King Solomon articulated God's desired relationship with humankind, "I love those who love me, and those who seek me diligently will find me," (Prov. 8:17).

---

*Time in His presence produces an insatiable thirst for His enlightenment and refreshing.*

---

While Mark 1:35 provided narrative on the importance of establishing a regular time and place in which to be with the Father, Matthew 14:13 reveals the occasional press of external circumstances which demand time apart from the rigors of life and ministry. "When Jesus heard it, He departed from there by boat to a deserted place by Himself," (v. 13). "The Aramaic word *khorba* means "uninhabited place." The Aramaic word for "the wilderness" is *madbra*, which means "a wasteland" or "a land without water or vegetation." Jesus went to an uninhabited place close to Tiberius."[89] Having heard of John the Baptist's execution, Jesus determined to be alone and to find a place where He could maintain privacy necessary to meet with His Father. Even the Son of God had to be intentional about His discipline in seeking solitude both as regularity with His Father and during times when life's circumstances signaled the need for additional solitary

---

[88] Merton, 261.

[89] George Mamishisho Lamsa, *More Light on the Gospel; Over 400 New Testament Passages Explained*, 1st ed. (Garden City: Doubleday, 1968), 20.

conversation with Him. Citing God's remoteness, George Arthur Buttrick admits, "The actual presence of God is often accompanied by a sense of his remoteness. One must speak to him if only to tell him how impossible it is to hold conversation with him. To those unaccustomed to spiritual experience this sounds like nonsense; to those to whom God is real it is the essence of divine-human interaction."[90] Buttrick rightly describes God's apparent remoteness to the leader who fails to establish a sense of discipline in his or her pursuit of the Father's presence. Additionally, leaders who maintain the discipline of solitude in proximity to the Father's heart find God to be faithful and revealing of His will. Time in His presence produces an insatiable thirst for His enlightenment and refreshing. The psalmist poignantly discloses, "As the deer pants for the water brooks, so pants my soul for you, O God. My soul thirsts for God, for the living God," (Ps. 42:1-2).

The desire to hear the heart of the Father needs to drive the effective leader into the quiet and solitary presence of a Father who manifests Himself publically only after revealing Himself privately. A regular presence with the Father produces human hearts capable of rightly discerning His voice and executing His will.

Only God's favor produces the influence necessary to lead effectively and only time spent in solitude with the Father produces that favor. Solitude provides the opportunity for the human spirit to sensitize to the will of God. Every other component of spiritual formation emanates from the

---

[90] George Arthur Buttrick, *The Interpreter's Bible: The Holy Scriptures in the King James and Revised Standard Versions with General Articles and Introduction, Exegesis, Exposition for Each Book of the Bible*, vol. 4 (New York: Abingdon-Cokesbury Press, 1951), 222.

heart of a loving and unfailing Father who wants only to impart those components to leaders who, in turn, produce leaders. Solitude is the most neglected discipline of the four (Solitude, Sabbatical, Solidarity, and Strategy). Leaders who neglect the discipline of Solitude opt to proceed without confidence of God's actual counsel and avoid possible personal course corrections intended for the leader's effectiveness.

.

CHAPTER 5

# Sabbatical : Staying Fresh

*Pastors and leaders who omit intentional rest or
downplay its necessary by-product of emotional balance
eventually face the decision of whether or not to continue.*

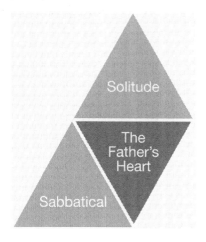

Among the many disciplines of spiritual leadership,
Sabbatical ranks near the top of the "most-difficult-to-keep"
list. The lack of sabbatical discipline as a regular component
in a leader's life promises to exact an eventual reckoning both
in terms of productivity and intentionality.[91] A driven work

---

[91] This chapter reveals that Sabbath keeping does not always mean
taking Sunday or Saturday as a day in which to observe Sabbath. The
discipline of Sabbatical includes the leader's option to integrate rest and
relaxation into his or her rhythm of life. Sabbatical can be a daily, weekly,
or monthly time set aside for the leader's personal benefit of mental,
physical, and spiritual recharging.

ethic can function as the enemy to a leader's ability to pace him or herself for the long haul that ministry entails. Additionally, the inspiration and energy level in which the leader operates begins to diminish to a point devoid of optimistic perspective and morphs into a pessimistic, maintenance expression of service. The prospect of continued ministry involvement evaporates like a cool mist on a hot day.

Noted author, pastor, and leader Wayne Cordeiro faced a near-fatal burnout episode from which he later emerged determined to realign the physical priorities that had sidelined him. He explains, "Your soul is like a battery that discharges each time you give life away, and it needs to be recharged regularly."[92] Cordeiro admonishes leaders to keep their "batteries" charged by regularly taking the necessary steps to ensure continued zeal for ministry and stamina to finish strong. Barton adds, "Sabbath keeping may be the most challenging rhythm for leaders to establish because Sunday in most churches has become a day of Christian busyness—and of course, the busiest person on that day is the pastor."[93] Together with the intrinsic quality of spiritual service, leaders often opt for overwork as a means by which their acceptance and validation gain a spiritual standing in the eyes of those they lead. Their misplaced perspective fuels the fire of heightened expectations and produces nothing except tired and uninspiring individuals intent on keeping the misperception alive. God intended for humankind to rest. He did not intend for rest to be considered idleness but rather an

---

[92] Wayne Cordeiro, *Leading on Empty: Refilling Your Tank and Renewing Your Passion* (Minneapolis: Bethany House, 2009), 88.

[93] Barton, 123.

essential component of balance for the human persona. Alan Fadling emphasizes the importance of seeking and maintaining a healthy balance: "Holy leisure and unholy idleness are polar opposites. This sort of idleness isn't life-giving. It isn't good. It isn't God's way. But I am recommending that we consider stepping off the treadmill or out of the fast lane long enough to relax and linger in God's presence, to walk with him at his pace."[94]

Pastors experience an adrenaline bombardment each weekend as they prepare for their main services and deliver carefully crafted messages aimed at soliciting either participation in church missional activities or convincing the congregant of the need for a deeper spiritual commitment. The after-effects of the increased adrenaline in their endocrine systems leave the pastors mildly depressed and emotionally fatigued. For that reason, many pastors opt to take Monday as their personal day and by Monday afternoon or evening, their mood returns to a normal range. The human body manufactures norepinephrine and serotonin— antidepressants that act as mood levelers. Increased levels of adrenaline have an adverse affect on these chemicals and can cause an imbalance leading to mild or severe depression.[95] Pastors and leaders who omit intentional rest or downplay its necessary by-product of emotional balance eventually face the decision of whether or not to continue.

Cordeiro points out, "No one is immune from the slow grip of depression when they are wrestling through a season

---

[94] Alan Fadling, *An Unhurried Life: Following Jesus' Rhythms of Work and Rest* (Downers Grove, IL: InterVarsity Press, 2013), 40.

[95] Lisa Stannard, "The Effects of Serotonin and Norepinephrine in Depression," *Livingstrong.com*, http://www.livestrong.com/article/73224-effects-serotonin-norepinephrine-depression/ (accessed September 10, 2012).

of burnout. More serious levels of depression that are accompanied by thoughts of suicide will require immediate attention."[96] Individuals who lead must eventually face the consequences of misplaced priorities that masquerade as legitimate expectations born of leadership.

The position for successful Sabbatical utilizes a venue that neutralizes overt demands and minimizes the leader's temptation to stay engaged in activity that depletes his or her energy reserve. A deliberate plan must drive the development of a Sabbatical mindset and provide an understanding of why God places so much value on the discipline. "The requirement of Sabbath observance invites us to stop. It invites us to rest. It asks us to notice that while we rest the world continues without our help. It invites us to find delight in the world's beauty and abundance."[97] Most pastors and other ministry leaders struggle with the idea of a regular time away and insist upon playing the odds against eventual physical burnout or ministerial dropout—or both. Hans Finzel avows, "Because of the intense demands on leaders, it is tempting to get out of balance in our personal lives. Many leaders fail in their professional lives because they lose control of their personal lives."[98]

Leaders must place themselves in the position of Sabbatical by intentionally removing themselves from the harness of duty and external expectation and letting God refresh and renew their entire being. Simply put, that means they must distance themselves from the pressures and responsibilities germane to their vocation and refresh their

---

[96] Cordeiro, 44.

[97] Norman Wirzba, *Living the Sabbath: Discovering the Rhythms of Rest and Delight, The Christian Practice of Everyday Life* (Grand Rapids: Brazos Press, 2006), 12.

[98] Finzel, 125.

inner person without allowing guilt to inflict its predictable salvo of debilitating bombs. A well-planned-for vacation is an option if it mandates the intentional disconnect from one's on-going application of his or her ministry venue and provides a clear-cut time of rest.

Sabbatical should shape the leader's life and calendar and become a regularly practiced discipline that guides the leader's attention to living within a safe margin that recognizes the individual's need to rest. Norman Wirzba states that, rather than being simply a "break" from frenetic, self-obsessed ways of living, the Sabbath is a discipline and practice in which leaders ask, consider, and answer the questions that will lead them into a complete and joyful life.[99] Sabbatical must not become a legalistic expression of something that works in another context, but the application of a personal truth designed by God to refresh each of His children. Cordeiro warns that an intentional life must include consistent times of monitoring and assessment so that the entropy associated with a mediocre lifestyle cannot superimpose itself on the child of God. He further states that everyone will sooner or later have to deal with fatigue in the midst of a demanding ministry unless time is set aside to rest and align with God's original design.[100] As the decades-old oil filter commercial stated, "You can pay me now or pay me later."[101] Simple engine maintenance promises to help prevent costly repair,

---

[99] Wirzba, 20.

[100] Wayne Cordeiro, *Leading on Empty: Refilling Your Tank and Renewing Your Passion* (Minneapolis: Bethany House, 2009), 166.

[101] Lawrence P. Farrell, Jr., "Pay Me Now or Pay Me Later," *National Defense Magazine*, December 2011, http://www.nationaldefensemagazine.org/archive/2011/December/DayofReckoningIsApproachingIt'sPayMeNoworPayMeLater.aspx (accessed April 10, 2013).

but if neglected, the end cost rises exponentially. Likewise, leaders pay a greater personal cost if they neglect the preventive maintenance of sabbatical.

---

*Sabbatical should shape the leader's life and calendar and become a regularly practiced discipline that guides the leader's attention to living within a safe margin that recognizes the individual's need to rest.*

---

The purpose of Sabbatical aims to once again draw into proximity with the Father and allow His strengthening and refreshing. Bob Sorge maintains that God's rest is available but not guaranteed. It becomes, as he calls it, a "secret place" where the leader uncovers God's rest "through a diligent pursuit of the secret place."[102] The leader must understand that purpose provides clarity of intent and determination to follow through with an intentional effort. Without having a purpose for something, little gets accomplished. Likewise, without understanding both the benefits and ramifications of Sabbatical, leaders fail to pace themselves to finish strong and increase the chances of physical, mental, and spiritual collapse.

God's rest can only be found in ceasing from works and learning simply to be in the presence of the Father (Heb. 4:10). He spoke directly to Moses admonishing him to "Speak also to the children of Israel, saying: Surely My Sabbaths you shall keep, for it is a sign between you throughout your generations, that you may know that I am the Lord who sanctifies you" (Exod. 31:13). God intended the Sabbath to allow people time to disconnect from everything that drained

---

[102] Bob Sorge, *Secrets of the Secret Place: Keys to Igniting Your Personal Time with God* (Lee's Summit, MO: Oasis House, 2001), 152.

# The Proximity Factor

them during the week, deliberately giving them permission to rest. Finzel reiterates, "I remember how hard it was to take those days away from my office—but looking back on it today, what could be more important? As we get older and look back on our lives, who says that they wish they had spent more time at the office?"[103]

Cordeiro implies that by working on the Sabbath, "we mistakenly convey that what we do during that time is as important as what God did at creation."[104] He further asserts, "The Sabbath is a declaration that God has finished his work of creation. No one needs to add to it, and no one should."[105] Wirzba insightfully posits, "When understood in its proper depth and breadth, the Sabbath not only situates us within the orders of creation, and thus within the larger drama of God's redeeming love, but also opens new paths as we journey toward justice, peace and joy."[106]

God had a purpose for instituting the Sabbath. He knew the propensity of humanity would always be to exhaust self and resources to maintain control over his or her life and future. Wirzba adds, "Sabbath frames our entire life, helping us set priorities and determine which of our activities and aspirations bring honor to God."[107] Sabbath provides a time in which leaders may ascertain if the major area of their concentration of time and effort really produces the intended result. Maintenance of a Sabbath time of rest produces an entirely different perspective in which individuals may gain a sense of God's intended rhythm of life and connectedness with Him. Wirzba reflects,

---

103 Finzel, 129.
104 Cordeiro, 184.
105 Ibid., 183.
106 Wirzba, 14.
107 Ibid., 23.

Sabbath is the time for us to relax and let down our guard, to pause from the often anxious and competitive patterns of daily life. As our most important and all-encompassing goal, it frames and contextualizes our planning, much as the desire to achieve a specific objective.[108]

Such a mentality eludes most of those who bear the weight of leadership as they seek to balance expectations of those they lead with the divine imperative to employ regular times of sabbatical. Unless the option for Sabbatical becomes the only option the leader embraces, the expectations of subordinates and superiors will continue to define the leader's application of his or her leadership gifts.

Sabbatical's process differs with each willing participant. Though some leaders feel that a large chunk of time away works best for them, others integrate smaller, neutral times into their schedules. Depending upon what truly replenishes the leader, most who eventually return to ministry following severe burnout easily understand and incorporate the practice as a vital part of his or her life. Some leaders opt for a planned-upon time away from their leadership contexts. Others wisely integrate sabbatical time into their weekly schedules. However, if they do not plan to implement Sabbatical into their work routines, they set themselves up for certain downtime in which they must face the prospect of emotional and spiritual burnout.

Sabbatical demands intentionality. Lauren Winner maintains that spiritual practices do not justify nor save us. Rather, they refine our Christianity. She adds an etymological clue in her assertion that practicing the spiritual disciplines

---

[108] Wirzba, 23.

teaches, "... what it means to live as Christians (*discipline* is related to the word *disciple*)."[109] Personal spiritual growth, especially in terms of leading effectively, demands the integration of the spiritual disciplines necessary to provide a conduit from which to receive wisdom, rest, absolution of guilt, and restoration from God.

---

## Sabbatical demands intentionality.

---

Sabbatical's product ensures both a rested heart capable of coming into the presence of God without the baggage of duty or guilt and a debris-free heart capable of giving Him undivided attention. The sooner a leader finds that "secret place," the sooner he or she finds God's place of refreshing. Its accomplishment demands intentionality and determination. The leader must rightly ascertain the importance of gaining the Father's presence and obtaining the subsequent refreshing that only comes from the deliberate disconnect with pressures inherent in his or her calling and function.

Charles Cowman, African missionary during the early part of the twentieth century, wrote:

> In the deep jungles of Africa, a traveler was making a long trek. Coolies had been engaged from a tribe to carry the loads. The first day they marched rapidly and went far. The traveler had high hopes of a speedy journey. But the second morning these jungle tribesmen refused to move. For some strange reason they just sat and rested. On inquiry as to the reason for

---

[109] Lauren F. Winner, *Mudhouse Sabbath* (Brewster, MS: Paraclete Press, 2003), xiii.

this strange behavior, the traveler was informed that they had gone too fast the first day, and that they were now waiting for their souls to catch up with their bodies. This whirling rushing life, in which so many of us live does for us what that first march did for those poor tribesmen. The difference: they knew what they needed to restore life's balance; too often, we do not.[110]

Sabbatical should be the goal of every leader who desires effectiveness in leadership and authenticity in his or her relationship with the Father. Proximity to the Father's heart produces new for old, fresh for stale, and transformation for crystallization. The Father promises to reinvigorate the tired and callous heart. "I will give you a new heart and put a new spirit within you; I will take the heart of stone out of your flesh and give you a heart of flesh" (Ezek. 36:26). He promises to replace anxiety with hope. "Anxiety in the heart of man causes depression, but a good word makes it glad" (Prov. 12:25). He promises that time spent in His presence will produce change in the heart of everyone who diligently seeks Him. "I love those who love me, and those who seek me diligently will find me" (Prov. 8:17).

---

*Sabbatical should be the goal of every leader who desires effectiveness in leadership and authenticity in his or her relationship with the Father.*

---

Diligence to the discipline of sabbatical carries the Father's guarantee that time spent listening to His heart produces everything the leader needs to be the kind of leader

---

[110] Charles E. Cowman and Oriental Missionary Society, *Springs in the Valley* (Los Angeles: Oriental Missionary Society, 1939), 196–197.

who in turn produces other leaders with a heart for the Father. As the discipline of sabbatical in the life of the leader develops, he or she discovers the wisdom produced by a rested body and uncluttered mind.

## A Theology of Sabbatical

The Creator, who, himself rested after six days of creation, built rest into the natural rhythms of life. Lillian Daniel succinctly states, "When God feels absent in my life, it usually means I am out of rhythm. As a pastor, when I hit a dark night of the soul, it is usually because I have not been spending enough dark nights asleep."[111] Rest and sleep fortify the leader's resolve to work productively and with the necessary energy level that leadership demands. A rested mind enters more easily into a time of solitude. As rest prepares the leader to think and act intentionally, times of solitude remain focused and alert to what the Father might say to an inquiring heart. "An important part of the meaning of rest is suggested by the mystery of divine rest: it draws a boundary around work and exertion and takes a legitimate delight in celebrating what has been accomplished, without an urge to keep working."[112] The Old Testament first records the institution of Sabbath in the laws of Moses in Exodus 16:22-30, and mandated a weekly day of rest.[113] Merrill expounds,

The fourth commandment, that having to do with

[111] Lillian Daniel, "Get Some Sleep, Establish Rhythm," *Leadership Journal* 2 (Fall 2011), under "Where I Find Refreshment," http://www.christianitytoday.com/le/2011/fall/findrefreshment.html (accessed September 3, 2013).

[112] Leland Ryken et al., *Dictionary of Biblical Imagery* (Downers Grove: InterVarsity Press, 1998), 709.

[113] David Noel Freedman, Allan C. Myers, and Astrid B. Beck. *Eerdmans Dictionary of the Bible* (Grand Rapids: Eerdmans, 2000), 1145.

Sabbath observance, is one of two commandments expressed in the affirmative. The commandment begins with an infinitival form of the verb *samar* that functions here as an imperative. With the following infinitive and preposition (*leqaddeso*), it forms a common oratory expression, "Watch carefully to keep it holy." The parallel in Exod. 20:8 also employs an infinitive absolute, but the verb is *zakar*, "remember," rather than *samar*.[114]

The Pentateuch presents two major rationales for Sabbath observance. "The concept of the Sabbath as a memorial to God's resting from the work of creation is expressed in Genesis 2:1-3 and repeated in Exodus 20:11 and 31:17. Although God had already sanctified the seventh day at the time of creation, God did not reveal its special status to humankind at large, but only to Israel."[115] God singled Israel out and provided directives designed to cause alignment with His greater purposes for the Jewish people. Lauren Winner explains, "There are, in Judaism, two types of commandments (*mitzvot*): the *mitzvot asei*, or the 'Thou shalts,' and the *mitzvot lo ta'aseh*, or the 'Thou shalt nots.'"[116] The discipline of sabbatical living laid the foundation for the Jewish people's ability to keep all the commandments.

Sabbath observance within the context of the Scriptures carried the weight of being a life or death matter. Moses put Sabbath observance at the top of the list of things God had

---

[114] Eugene H. Merrill, *Deuteronomy*, The New American Commentary 4 (Nashville: Broadman & Holman, 1994), 150.

[115] James Luther Mays, Joseph Blenkinsopp, eds., *The HarperCollins Bible Dictionary*, 3rd ed., rev. and updated (New York: HarperCollins, 2011), 900.

[116] Lauren F. Winner, *Mudhouse Sabbath* (Brewster: Paraclete Press, 2003), 4.

commanded them to do: "Six days work shall be done, but on the seventh day you shall have a holy Sabbath of solemn rest for the Lord; whoever does any work on it shall be put to death" (Exod. 35:2). The Hebrew word *sabbat* meant "to cease or desist" for the weekly day of rest and abstention from work enjoined upon the Israelites.[117] Sabbath rest was buttressed by a system of festivals that constituted an important part of Hebrew religious life.[118] "Another part of the symbolism of Sabbath rest was that it pictured release from the bondage of Israel in Egypt (Deut. 5:15). Rest is a form of freedom—from work, from human striving and acquisitiveness, from worldly preoccupations."[119] Over time, strict observance of the Sabbath produced a sense of willing compliance among those liberated from the toils associated with their slavery. Exodus 20:8-11 reiterates directives for Sabbath observance in the context of commandments relating to God.

> Remember the Sabbath day, and keep it holy. Six days you shall labor and do all your work. But the seventh day is a Sabbath to the Lord your God; you shall not do any work--you, your son or your daughter, your male of female slave, your livestock, or the alien resident in your towns. For in six days the Lord made heaven and earth, the sea and all that is in them, but rested the seventh day; therefore the Lord blessed the Sabbath day and consecrated it (NRSV).

The commandment pertaining to the Sabbath (Exod. 20:8, "Remember the Sabbath day to keep it holy") stipulated

---

[117] Mays and Blenkinsopp, 900.
[118] Ryken, 709.
[119] Ibid., 710.

that, while other days provided opportunity to carry on the duties of everyday life, the Sabbath became a day set apart for Yahweh, as other days were, "profane or secular."[120] "Once the Sabbath had been instituted, specific commands and prohibitions were given. The Sabbath was not only a day of rest, but also a feast day. Because of this, the requirements of feast days were enforced, including holy convocations, public worship, and worship in the home."[121] The Israelites considered it a joy and blessing but also maintained its sacred intent. "Some scholars insist that its original form was negative, such as the following: 'you shall not do any work on the Sabbath day.' In origin it was a taboo day, on which work was forbidden, rather than a day for religious festival."[122] While the original intent of the commandment insured the Israelites give Yahweh due respect and worship, it also became a day in which they actually rested from their toils and allowed the rhythm of their lives to be shaped by the priority of the Sabbath.

Contemporary societal expectations for Sabbath observance pale in comparison to the sabbatical rhythm established by God in His dealing with the people of Israel. Modern cultures seem to honor competitive work over the discipline of rest. Additionally, modern families struggle with financial standards required maintaining a style of living— often driven by materialism and the drive to maintain at least an average standard of living. For that reason, many families need two incomes to sustain a reasonable existence—often to the neglect of a day of rest. The prophet Isaiah articulated

---

[120] J. Philip Hyatt, *Exodus*, New Century Bible Commentary (Grand Rapids: Eerdmans, 1980), 213.

[121] Freedman, Myers, and Beck, 1145.

[122] Hyatt, 213.

God's intended benefit for instituting the Sabbath rest:

> If you turn away your foot from the Sabbath, from doing your pleasure on my holy day, and call the Sabbath a delight, the holy day of the Lord honorable, and shall honor Him, not doing your own ways, nor finding your own pleasure, nor speaking your own words, then you shall delight yourself in the Lord; And I will cause you to ride on the high hills of the earth, and feed you with the heritage of Jacob your father. The mouth of the Lord has spoken (Isa. 58:13-14).

---

## Sabbatical living should shape one's life rhythm and calendar.

---

This chapter emphasizes that sabbatical living should characterize the life of anyone determined to pace him or herself for the entirety of life's journey. Sabbatical living should shape one's life rhythm and calendar. Naturally, one might ask, "How legalistic should a person be in observing the challenge to sabbatical living?" Jesus garnered the rebuke of the Pharisees for picking grain form the field on Shabbat. He criticized those trying to enforce a fetish of Sabbath observance when He said, "the Sabbath was made for man, not man for the Sabbath," (Mark 2:27). "Rather than being simply a 'break' from frenetic, self obsessed ways of living, the Sabbath is a discipline and practice in which we ask, consider, and answer the questions that will lead us into a complete and joyful life."[123] Sabbatical living provides a "margin" in which a leader can evaluate his or her adherence

---

[123] Norman Wirzba, *Living the Sabbath: Discovering the Rhythms of Rest and Delight*, The Christian Practice of Everyday Life (Grand Rapids: Brazos Press, 2006), 20.

to misplaced priorities or unfruitful activities and make the necessary course corrections.

The whole premise of Sabbath insists one looks outside familiar insight and allows the actual discipline of rest to permeate work and activity—providing a suitable balance to the frenzied pace currently associated with most lives. "Practicing the spiritual disciplines does not make us Christians. Instead, the practicing teaches us what it means to live as Christians. (There is an etymological clue here— *discipline* is related to the word *disciple*.)"[124] The essential goal of leadership must be to be shaped by the process of discipline. John Orton states, "A disciple of Jesus is simply someone who seeks to have their spirit formed by him. If you are interested in Christian spiritual formation, the way you pursue it is by becoming a disciple of Jesus."[125] To be a disciple of Jesus means to be willing and determined to pursue the necessary course change in being a vessel that God can use in His plan to reach all humankind. Quick fixes and shortcuts only lengthen the desired process of personal transformation—especially if the leader neglects the discipline of rest.

"Sabbath frames our whole life and helps us set priorities and determine which of our activities and aspirations bring honor to God."[126] Sabbatical living mandates a re-prioritizing of events that keep us from the presence of the Father. If an individual cannot learn how to rest and live with margin (sabbatical) he or she cannot experience true solitude in

---

[124] Winner, xiii.

[125] John Ortberg, "Seven Things I Hate About Spiritual Formation," *Leadership Journal* (April 2013): 2.

[126] Wirzba, 23.

proximity to the Father's heart. The fact that Sabbath observance has a low priority for many people in our society indicates a profound confusion about what the Sabbath means. Wirzba echoes the words of Jesus in Mark 2:27 as he points out, "It ought to be our highest priority and our deepest desire, because the experience of delight is what the Sabbath is all about."[127] Merrill adds, "There is more to Sabbath observance than mere recollection of the past or even determination to conform; there must be a studied effort to keep the day holy, an actual involvement in its requirements and prohibitions."[128] Barton piques the leader's interest: "Sabbath keeping is a discipline that will mess with you, because once you move beyond just thinking about it and actually begin to practice it, the goodness of it will capture you, body, soul and spirit."[129]

Matthew records the classic biblical invitation to find the valued venue of rest in the presence Jesus Christ: "Come to Me, all you who labor and are heavy laden, and I will give you rest. Take My yoke upon you and learn from Me, for I am gentle and lowly in heart, and you will find rest for your souls. For My yoke is easy and My burden is light" (11:28-30). Jesus related that the source of His inspirational invitation to find His rest came from His Father. His invitation to live in daily sabbatical laid the foundation for all determined to live within close proximity to the Father's heart.

While Psalm 91 describes the blessings and benefits of abiding, "under the shadow of the Almighty," (v. 1), Psalm 92 provides a good sequel. Having followed the advice of Psalm 91, the psalmist provides a narrative introducing Psalm 92 as

127 Ibid., 52.
128 Merrill, 150.
129 Barton, *Sacred Rhythms*, 133.

a "Song for the Sabbath Day." Wirzba points out, "When our work and our play, our exertion and our rest flow seamlessly from this deep desire to give thanks to God, the totality of our living—cooking, eating, cleaning, preaching, teaching, parenting, building, repairing, healing, creating—becomes one sustained and ever-expanding act of worship."[130] The Bible does not provide an alternative to the discipline of sabbatical living. The wisdom of God and the frailty of humanity require adherence to the biblical discipline of employing disconnect from the pressures and burdens of life.

Sabbath keeping is more than just taking a day of rest; it is a way of ordering one's life around a pattern of working six days and then resting on the seventh. It is a way of arranging our life to honor the rhythm of things—work and rest, fruitfulness and dormancy, giving and receiving, being and doing, activism and surrender.[131]

The practice of a regular Sabbath day may not culturally fit current sociological demands, but living in the discipline of sabbatical becomes a viable alternative to taking a whole day every week to disconnect. While the Sabbath is a "sacramental" day, "it reminds us week by week of the Sabbath satisfaction that God knows in eternity (Gen. 2:3), and which He seeks to share with us in the here and now."[132] Leaders who incorporate sabbatical living into their daily regimen find a greater sense of the Father's presence because they place the rest sabbatical provides as a top priority— insuring both spiritual and physical longevity. Psalm 116 echoes the heart of a leader who has discovered the value of

---

[130] Wirzba, 21.

[131] Barton, *Sacred Rhythms*, 134.

[132] George Angus Fulton Knight, *Psalms* (Philadelphia: Westminster Press, 1982), 98.

sabbatical living: "Return to your rest, O my soul, for the Lord has dealt bountifully with you," (v. 7). Effective leadership emerges from daily times of rest in which the leader discovers the irreplaceable resource found only in proximity to the Father's heart. A daily discipline of sabbatical translates to higher productivity in all the leader does and helps provide an anxiety-free heart more capable of hearing the Father's heart during times of solitude. The two disciplines must go together.

The obvious first choice for Sabbath would be a weekly-designated time in which the leader does absolutely nothing but rest. However, that possibility finds great difficulty in its implementation in the context of current culture. The next most obvious choice emerges from a schedule the leader determines will include regular sabbatical living in which he or she deliberately cordons off time to effectively disconnect from external pressures intent on dictating the leader's pace of life.

---

*A daily discipline of sabbatical translates to higher productivity in all the leader does and helps provide an anxiety-free heart more capable of hearing the Father's heart during times of solitude. The two disciplines must go together.*

---

During some of his most weary and trying times, David penned, "Oh that I had wings like a dove! For then I would fly away and be at rest," (55:6). Another time he wrote, "Rest in the Lord, and wait patiently for Him," (37:7). He knew that true rest did not just happen on its own accord, but had to be a deliberate effort by the one needing to enter into rest. Yet, he knew the sustaining power of rest to the weary soul. That knowledge carried him through the formative years of his leadership as God declared David to be, "a man after My own heart" (Acts 13:22).

---

*The wisdom of God and the frailty of humanity require adherence to the biblical discipline of employing disconnect from the pressures and burdens of life.*

---

The prophet Isaiah spoke of rest in a historical context for the nation of Israel. He revealed the hearts of the people when he said, "this is the rest with which You (God) may cause the weary to rest, and this is the refreshing, yet they would not hear," (Isa. 28:12; 30:15). "The *rest* carries the connotations of dwelling and of the secure condition of that residence. The verse builds a beautiful chiasmus of five lines which portray Yahweh's original offer to Israel of 'rest' in Canaan and her responsibility to *give rest to the weary* there."[133] Isaiah described the conditions surrounding Ephraim's hardheartedness and the resultant absence of rest that God had promised them. The people made a covenant with death (v. 15) and had resigned themselves to living out that fate. The prophet Jeremiah made a similar plea to the inhabitants of Jerusalem. "This says the Lord: Stand in the ways and see, and ask for the old paths, where the good way is, and walk in it; Then you will find rest for your souls. But they said, 'We will not walk in it,'" (Jere.6:16). An historical overview of the nation of Israel reveals the result of their hardened hearts and stubborn refusal to enter God's "rest." They spent a lot of time alienated from the promise God made to them because they refused to recognize God's desire for their obedience

---

[133] John D. W Watts, *Isaiah. 1-33*, Word Biblical Commentary 24 (Waco: Word Books, 1985), 364.

and fellowship.

Spiritual formation demands a willingness to enter the rest of the Lord. While each leader's "rest" may not have national or international implications, he or she must still determine to accept the resource God offers His children. "The requirement of Sabbath observance invites us to stop. It invites us to rest. It asks us to notice that while we rest the world continues without our help. It invites us to find delight in the world's beauty and abundance."[134] It allows the leader to enjoy the instructive times that come from being in close proximity to the Father's heart. The Apostle Paul offered encouragement to early believers who encountered regular persecution. He simply invited those who were troubled to rest so the stress of their afflictions might not diminish their zeal (2 Thess. 1:7). The word "rest" comes from the Greek word *enesis,* which means "to let up, to relax, to stop being stressed, or to find relief."[135] The picture of the release of a bowstring under great pressure illustrates the intended transition from stress to rest. "The point of the Sabbath is to honor our need for a sane rhythm of work and rest. It begins with a willingness of acknowledge the limits of our humanness and take steps to live more graciously within the order of things."[136]

The Apostle Paul also illustrates the power of the indwelling Spirit of God. "But if the Spirit of Him who raised Jesus from the dead dwells in you, He who raised Christ from the dead will also give life to your mortal bodies through His Spirit who dwells in you," (Rom. 8:11). Paul's phrase "give

---

[134] Wirzba, 12.

[135] Rick Renner, *Sparkling Gems from the Greek: 365 Greek Word Studies for Every Day of the Year to Sharpen Your Understanding of God's Word* (Tulsa, OK: Teach All Nations, 2003), Kindle e-book, locations 3838–3842.

[136] Barton, *Sacred Rhythms,* 137.

life" comes from the Greek word *zoopoieo*, originating from the words *zoe* and *poieo*. The word *zoe* is the Greek word for life and it often describes the life of God. The word *poieo* means "to do." When compounded together it means "to make alive with life."[137] The verse infers the supernatural infusion of God's Spirit upon the human spirit produces revitalization during difficult episodes in which the leader finds proximity to the Father's heart essential for life.

The promised rest (Matt. 11:28) offers the invitation to respond to mental, physical, and spiritual rest rooted in the unshakable promises of Jesus Christ. A rested heart enters more easily into the proximity of the Father's heart than does a weary heart. The goal of solitude eludes the individual who neglects the discipline of rest as an over-riding rhythm of life. The Father knows the limitations of a weary heart and He desires greatly to impart His restorative touch to the individual who will allow Him the time to thoroughly discern the thoughts and intentions of their heart (Heb. 4:12).

## How does a rested heart (sabbatical) improve our ability to listen to God (solitude)?

We cannot hope to enjoy spiritual bliss if our life is characterized by pain and distress. The disappointments of life provide ample reason to be skeptical. It goes with the territory of being human. The **good news** is that we don't have to go it alone. It was our Lord and Master who said,

*"Come to me, all you who are weary and burdened, and I will give you rest. [29] Take my yoke upon you and learn from me, for I am gentle and humble in heart, and you*

---

[137] Renner, locations 8273–8278.

*will find rest for your souls. [30] For my yoke is easy and my burden is light." Matthew 11:28-30*

So, how does one begin to segue from a hurried and haggard existence to being able to discern the voice of God? How does a person begin to sense he or she can actually hear the heart of the Father? Remember, I said that this book does not dispense theory nor does it embrace platitudes that have no origin from close proximity to the Father's heart.

Let me draw a picture for you. I love a large city's Botanical Center. You can walk in a controlled environment and wander among the tropical vegetation. There is real peace there. I used to take a sack lunch and just sit in the serene surroundings and think. Those were the days when cell phones were still just a fad and nobody took them seriously.

When I speak of a garden, think about the Botanical Center. If your city has a Botanical Center, visit it and take your time to soak in the peace and quiet. You will be amazed at the level of inner peace and tranquility produced by your visit there.

There are two places in which we meet with God. One is what I call the **tabernacle**. I call the other one the **garden**. It is essential to our growth in Christ to be familiar with both places. As Gordon MacDonald called his place of meditation with Christ his "spiritual center," I call mine my "garden." It demands both a systematic cultivation and a regular visit.

Howard Rutledge, a United States Air Force pilot, was shot down over North Viet Nam during the early stages of the war. He spent several miserable years in the hands of his captors before being released at the war's conclusion. In his book, In the Presence of Mine Enemies, he reflects upon the resources from which he drew in those arduous days when life seemed so intolerable. He wrote,

"During those longer periods of enforced reflection it became so much easier to separate the important from the trivial, the worthwhile from the waste. For example, in the past, I usually worked or played hard on Sundays and had no time for church. For years Phyllis had encouraged me to join the family at church. She never nagged or scolded—she just kept hoping. But I was too busy, too preoccupied, to spend one or two short hours a week thinking about the really important things.

Now the sights and sounds and smells of death were all around me. My hunger for spiritual food soon outdid my hunger for a steak. Now I wanted to know about that part of me that will never die. Now I wanted to talk about God and Christ and the church. But in Heartbreak, (the name the POW's gave their prison camp) solitary confinement, there was no pastor, no Sunday School teacher, no Bible, no hymnbook, no community of believers to guide and sustain me. I had completely neglected the spiritual dimension of my life. It took prison to show me how empty life is without God."

I want you to discover your garden. It is essential that you discover that **place**, for it is the place of God's nourishment and feeding upon which you must center your life. Mr. Rutledge came to his garden with great difficulty. He was forced to examine things in his spiritual life that were not previously important to him. If we are to develop a spiritual life that gives contentment and restores spiritual passion, it will be because we approach spiritual living as a discipline, much as the athlete trains his body for competition.

I already alluded to what I call my "garden." It is there that my spiritual passion is rekindled. David (Psalms) was thinking in metaphors when he imagined his inner spirit to be like a pasture where God, the shepherd, led him as a lamb. In his metaphor there are calm waters, green pastures, and tables loaded with food to be eaten in safety.

---

*The Father communicates his peace to a listening heart. It is in the garden that we need not be concerned with being heard.*

---

For me, the garden is a place where the Spirit of God comes to make self-disclosure, to share wisdom, to give affirmation or rebuke, to provide encouragement, and to give direction and guidance. When this garden is in order, it is a quiet place, and there is an absence of busyness, of defiling noise and confusion. It becomes a place where rest comes easily and prepares the human heart for proximity to the heart of the Father. It underscores the importance of understanding how solitude and sabbatical go together and how importantly they serve as foundational stones in the spiritual formation of the effective leader.

Let's continue with an illustration designed to help the leader distinguish between differing activities during times of praise and prayer. Let me draw a comparison between the **tabernacle** and the **garden**. The **Tabernacle** is a picture of man coming into the presence of God (at His invitation) with conditions. It is a place where man has prepared to give to God. Man does all the talking (praise and worship) and God receives from us. The **Garden** is a picture of God coming into our presence (at our invitation). It is a place where God is prepared to give to man because God does all the talking and man does all the listening. **Both** become places of overflow.

> *"For as the soil makes the sprout come up and a garden causes seeds to grow, so the Sovereign Lord will make righteousness and praise spring up before all nations."*
> *Isaiah 61:11*

**Tabernacle overflow:**
1. Our praise and adoration from the cleanliness of our heart;
2. It is called a sacrifice of worship because it is often difficult to worship after coming into His presence after being out in the world. We **need** to be there!

**Garden overflow:**
1. Of His abundant watering;
2. Of His love and direction;
3. Our understanding of His purposes in our lives;

The Father communicates his peace to a listening heart. It is in the garden that we need not be concerned with being heard. The Father meets with his children one by one. There are no lines. It is a private place. There are no phones. He speaks to his children about what displeases Him in a gentle yet convincing way and tells them how wonderfully they are gifted. He helps us to see that our presence in the garden pleases Him immensely. We come away realizing that there is only one place where we can actually meet with God in reality. It is the place where He talks and we listen. It is a protected place. He who is in control of the universe is in control of the garden. No dogs allowed. Nothing to spoil the setting.

The trip to the garden is our responsibility. He will meet us there but will not take us there. The restoration of one's spiritual passion must include regular times in the garden of his peace—close to the Father's heart. Here are a few tips to getting there more often:

1. Find the route to the garden and go there often;
2. Go to the garden for advice on even the smallest matters;
3. Learn to live the attitude learned in the garden;
4. Identify obstacles that were effective in making you lose your way to the garden.

---

*The Father communicates his peace to a listening heart. It is in the garden that we need not be concerned with being heard.*

---

# CHAPTER 6

# The Discipline of Solidarity: Staying Connected

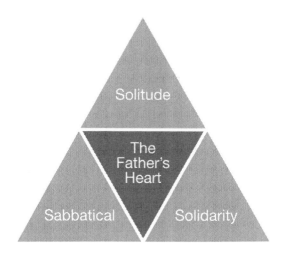

The term "Solidarity" identifies the third essential component of personal spiritual formation in the Proximity Factor. Solidarity is the "Unity (as of a group or class) that produces or is based on a community of interests, objectives, and standards; a feeling of unity between people who have the same interests, goals, etc."[138] If spiritual formation requires Solitude and Sabbatical in proximity to the Father's heart, Solidarity should also exist in the same proximity. Solidarity exists within the resourceful community of like-minded leaders who trust the relational aspect of collaboration with people capable of speaking into their lives and who, in turn, find proximity to the Father's heart a

---

[138] *The Merriam-Webster Dictionary*, s.v. "Solidarity."

requirement for effective life and leadership. A resourceful partnership with individuals sharing the same passion for personal leadership can provide an objective perspective needed to guide the leader's objectivity and perception of how God works in his or her life. John Price elaborates,

> God did not create faith, reason, and works as independent mechanisms to function in isolation to cover the various challenges people face. Instead, He crafted an elaborate interdependent system in which each component fills both distinct and collaborative roles. In keeping with God's design for free will, individuals may choose not to coordinate these activities or may neglect the function of individual components.[139]

Relational community provides a myriad of resources for leaders intent on becoming the quality of leader God designed. Connection is important in every area of life. Relationships are "more important than your position."[140] Connection with credible people provides insight and direction from an objective, yet vested point of view. People capable of discerning how the Father views the development of His leaders provide a glimpse of what they perceive as a weakness or strength in the leader. Every effective leader maintains a mental list of people they trust and deem capable of giving input into his or her life. "The Lord can and will provide a variety of covenant relationships throughout the seasons of our lives, which may include

---

[139] John Price, "Unifying Leadership: Bridging the Theory and Practice Divide," *Journal of Strategic Leadership* 3, no. 2 (Winter 2011): 14.

[140] Ron Hunter and Michael E. Waddell, *Toy Box Leadership: Leadership Lessons from the Toys You Loved as a Child* (Nashville: Thomas Nelson, 2008), 5.

spouses, key friends, family members, partners, mentors, and coaches."[141] Both professional and social context provides the arena in which solidarity can emerge and be a seminal ingredient of a leader's spiritual formation. Dallas Willard emphasizes, "Spiritual formation, good or bad, is always profoundly social. You cannot keep it to yourself. Anyone who thinks of it as a merely private matter has misunderstood it."[142] Spiritual formation includes, "…the progressive integration of who we are, of ourselves with the rest of creation, of our relationships, and of aesthetics."[143]

*Solidarity exists within the resourceful community of like-minded leaders who trust the relational aspect of collaboration with people capable of speaking into their lives and who, in turn, find proximity to the Father's heart a requirement for effective life and leadership.*

Leaders must connect with a relational community in which they can hear the Father's heart beating through other individuals who make hearing God a priority. Their positions must allow them to place themselves in a relationship in which the wisdom and experience of another helps guide them toward their eventual spiritual formation. "Listen to *counsel* and receive instruction, that you may be *wise* in your latter days" (Prov. 19:20; emphasis added). Paul Petit posits that spiritual formation is the ongoing process of the triune

[141] Joseph L. Umidi, *Transformational Coaching: Bridge Building That Impacts, Connects, and Advances the Ministry and the Marketplace* (n.p.: Xulon Press, 2005), 142.

[142] Dallas Willard, *Renovation of the Heart: Putting on the Character of Christ* (Colorado Springs: NavPress, 2002), 182.

[143] Mel Lawrenz, *The Dynamics of Spiritual Formation: Ministry Dynamics for a New Century Series* (Grand Rapids: Baker Books, 2000), 34.

God transforming the believer's life and character toward the life and character of Jesus Christ—accomplished by the ministry of the Spirit in the context of biblical community.[144] Leaders intent on the development of their ability to hear from God must realize the resourceful partnership capable of existence within relationships with friends, mentors, and other spiritual leaders. "The call to solidarity always moves us from exclusion to inclusion in order to embrace a greater mystery and a larger community. The movement from exclusive to inclusive community calls for radical hospitality, spiritual intimacy, and open communion in the Body of Christ."[145]

---

*Leaders must connect with a relational community in which they can hear the Father's heart beating through other individuals who make hearing God a priority.*

---

The subsequent spiritual development from collaborative input shapes their destiny and helps them to define the expression of their leadership gifts. While the collaboration from credible and trusted individuals provides opportunity for personal growth, they must also live in proximity to the Father's heart. Solidarity can diffuse the Father's message if leaders continually allow their spiritual formation to be shaped by someone who neglects input from their own time of solitude with the Father.

Walter Wright sees leadership as a relationship in which one person seeks to influence the thoughts, behaviors, beliefs,

---

[144] Pettit, 24.

[145] Henri J. M. Nouwen, *Spiritual Formation: Following the Movements of the Spirit*, 1st ed. (New York: HarperOne, 2010), 90.

or values of another person and that makes a difference.[146] A healthy relationship allows for the inter-relationship to exist as a bi-directional benefit to both parties involved. Wright further insists that it is time to celebrate shared relationships and balance un-centered lives with people who care, from family and friends to mentors and small groups.[147] Paul Leavenworth believes that healthy mentoring needs the essential element of empowerment, which "… involves transformational relationships in which all participants come to a healthier understanding and experience of their God-given potential as individuals, members of social networks, and members of a community who serve and empower others."[148] The spiritual formation of a leader demands the integration of counsel from men and women who rightly perceive God's perspective and who intentionally seek to apply it. Joseph L. Umidi avows that healthy, effective leaders proactively cultivate empowering relationships in every season of life.[149] Tony Stoltzfus writes, "We tend to think of the different kinds of soil as different kinds of people, but they can also represent different moments in our lives. In certain circumstances and with certain people, we are much more receptive to God's voice than we are elsewhere."[150]

Since ineffective leaders tend to move ahead in major decisions before receiving a word of guidance,[151] the issue of objective and spiritually motivated input requires an

---

[146] Wright, 2.

[147] Ibid., 8.

[148] Richard Clinton and Paul Leavenworth, *Living and Leading Well* (Des Moines: Convergence Publishing, 2012), 198.

[149] Umidi, 143.

[150] Tony Stoltzfus, *Leadership Coaching: The Disciplines, Skills and Heart of a Coach* (Virginia Beach: T. Stoltzfus, 2005), 35.

[151] J. Robert Clinton, *The Making of a Leader* (Colorado Springs: NavPress, 1988), 146.

intentional step by the leader to develop a constellation of counselors capable of raising his or her level of leadership. From the outset of the leader's decision to employ the wisdom and insights of like-minded people or professionals in a similar vocational venue, that leader must recognize his or her deficit of insight and be willing to have an open heart in response to whatever voice speaks into his or her life. "The word *heart*, as it appears in the Bible, refers to the core of our inner being in its fullness of mind, emotion and will. It is the essence of personality, the seat of all motives. The very intent of the word is to point to integration."[152] The purpose of solidarity becomes a collaborative effort in which the leader gains insights, perspective, and accountability through the spiritual formation of another.

---

*The impact of a mentor or coach provides traction in the leader's emergence into effective leadership and understanding of a broader leadership pattern.*

---

When leaders open their hearts to a change of perspective, they must grasp the wisdom of counsel germane to the issue at hand and realize God's provision of "skilled craftsmen" (Exod. 36:4) to assist in their spiritual formation. Umidi points out that formation involves transformation (*morphe*), which is a change in the inner person or essence. Those who will have the most transformational impact in lives will themselves need to be in transformational relationships that provide refreshing to them.[153] The solidarity of resourceful community with "skilled craftsmen" who can take the leader to the next level of personal and spiritual

---

[152] Lawrenz, *The Dynamics of Spiritual Formation*, 35.
[153] Umidi, 11.

development warrants intentional cultivation. The impact of a mentor or coach provides traction in the leader's emergence into effective leadership and understanding of a broader leadership pattern. Leavenworth provides a list outlining the characteristics of effective mentors:

- Ability to see potential in others;
- Tolerance of mistakes, brashness, abrasiveness, etc. in order to see potential developed;
- Flexibility in responding to people and circumstances;
- Patience, knowing that time and experience are needed for a person to develop potential;
- Perspective, having vision and ability to see down the road;
- Gifts and abilities to build up and encourage people.[154]

---

*The spiritual formation of a leader demands the integration of counsel from men and women who rightly perceive God's perspective and who intentionally seek to apply it.*

---

Bobb Biehl gives a historical perspective on the process of mentoring. The input from those who had gone before becomes a welcomed bridge to personal spiritual development. "In the past, mentoring happened everywhere. Mentoring was the chief learning method in the society of artisans where an apprentice spent years at the side of the craftsman learning not only the mechanics of a function, but the 'way of life' which surrounded it."[155] He further

---

[154] Clinton and Leavenworth, *Living and Leading Well*, 193.
[155] Bobb Biehl, *Mentoring: Confidence in Finding a Mentor and Becoming One* (Nashville: Broadman & Holman Publishers, 1996), 9.

comments on the state of present-day leadership. "Today, what passes for people development happens in a class room, and the certification of a person is by diploma from an institution rather than the stamp of approval from an overseer, a mentor."[156] The personal investment of a mentor in the life of a willing protégé provides opportunity for downloading gained wisdom and experience. A mentor who understands the process of exchange does not seek to replicate him or herself in the one being mentored, but utilizes the experience gained to broaden the protégé's perspective. A wise mentor sees both the limitations and the possibilities of the relationship.

---

*The personal investment of a mentor in the life of a willing protégé provides opportunity for downloading gained wisdom and experience.*

---

Fred Smith clarifies that mentors understand they are building "unique individuals," not imitators of themselves.[157] When a leader avails him or herself to the process of giving and gaining through the mentoring process, "God will confirm significant truth upon which a leader acts from more than one source in order to give credibility to leadership."[158] Mentoring provides the bridge that will connect, strengthen, and stabilize future generations of Christians in an increasingly complex and threatening world.[159] Smith also points out that a good mentor can see the hesitation of will, the nervousness of lost poise, the indecision of movement,

---

[156] Ibid.,10.
[157] Fred Smith, *You and Your Network: Getting the Most Out of Life* (Waco, TX: Word Books, 1984), 99.
[158] Clinton, *The Making of a Leader*, 147.
[159] Biehl, 15.

the tediousness of practice, and the despair of meaninglessness, or the boredom from lack of challenge.[160] The mentor relates from a personal context of experience gained through a lifetime of learning.

The mentor observes the potential in a leader and actively seeks to encourage the leader to develop the spiritual disciplines necessary to become an effective agent of change. The mandate of spiritual formation fuels the compliance with the growth process. Additionally, the mentor equips, empowers, and eventually emancipates the protégé to demonstrate the leadership disciplines he or she has developed through the course of time spent with the mentor as a result of sharing a common philosophy of life.[161]

> *God designed relational community to be a safe venue in which the exchange of ideas, inspiration, instruction, and vision could take place.*

The benefits of relational community (solidarity) also include leadership coaching. A coach is a change expert who helps leaders take responsibility for their lives and act to maximize their own potential through a system of accountability and challenge.[162] The coach collaborates with the leader and seeks to develop a relationship of trust. Kouzes and Posner posit, "Knowing trust is key, exemplary leaders make sure that they consider alternative viewpoints, and they make use of other people's expertise and abilities."[163] The stronger the trust, the stronger the influence of the coach

[160] Fred Smith, 101.
[161] Ibid., 95.
[162] Stoltzfus, 7.
[163] James M. Kouzes and Barry Z. Posner, *The Leadership Challenge* (San Francisco: Jossey-Bass, 2007), 247.

upon the leader. "In healthy leadership and healthy relationships, authority and responsibility go together. Since the authority to decide rests with the client (leader), a coach must function by influence, not by existing authority."[164] Solidarity emerges through trust gained and fruitful relationships established. As the process of solidarity becomes more defined in the life of the leader, the product also becomes more apparent. The leader experiences the necessary change needed to effectively segue from protégé to mentor or coach.

The product of leadership coaching must result in the transformation of the leader. "A transformational coach calls forth the heart to become alive and awakened to the reality of our true identity, and then allows the coaching process to unbind us and let us live that out in a way that causes the breakthrough."[165] Umidi avows that transformational learning (from solidarity with a coach) is learning that changes who a person is, not just what they do. He further adds,

> Transformational coaching bridges can and must be traversed by those who understand the transformational process and those who would raise up leadership for the next decade and beyond—leaders who will finish well, leaders who will lead well, and leaders who will leave a legacy of transformed lives because of the way they communicate the heart of God and their own hearts to those they are raising up.[166]

The product of solidarity reveals an individual capable of knowing he or she has heard form the Father's heart through

---

[164] Stoltzfus, 28.
[165] Umidi, 28.
[166] Ibid., 53.

the insightful and spiritually targeted input of the coach. Paul Petit states, "As individuals are conformed to Christ with an integrated devotion and within the community, they do not lose their individuality."[167] Solidarity provides the context in which personal spiritual formation may take place. Through the impact of living in relational community with coaches and mentors capable of facilitating growth in others, the Father's heart echoes His desire for spiritual formation in the leaders He called. Gordon Fee qualifies God's purpose in solidarity when he states, "God is not just saving individuals and preparing them for heaven; He is creating a people among whom He can live and who in their life together will reproduce God's life and character."[168] Stoltzfus cites that the reason Christians in general experience so little transformation in their lives resides in the fact that they, "ignore the Bible's relational mandate for how to affect change."[169] Relationship born of time spent with the Father provides the foundation upon which the coach may impact the life of the effective leader.

*The leader who fails to develop relational connections offers no prospect for the transformative value of solidarity.*

Spiritual maturity points to all God uses to bring His people (and leaders) into maturity capable of rightly discerning His heart's desire to redeem the lost. Paul Pettit summarizes his personal perspective on the purpose and product of solidarity. "Spiritual formation is far from a

---

[167] Pettit, 48.
[168] Gordon D. Fee, *Paul, the Spirit, and the People of God* (Peadbody, MA: Hendrickson Publishers, 1996), 66.
[169] Stoltzfus, 29.

private exercise between God and myself as an individual believer. Though he does the work in me, it is never just for my benefit…but as ambassadors of renewal for others, encouragement for the edification of other believers, and as witness of light to those who sit in darkness."[170] The spiritual formation of the leader must hold as its goal the transformation of others within the Christian community and within the world he or she is called to reach for Christ. John Donne, English poet and writer, expresses what he deems the purpose for all humankind:

> No man is an Island, entire of itself; every man is a piece of the Continent, a part of the main; if a clod be washed away by the sea, Europe is the less, as well as if a promontory were, as well as if a manor of thy friends or of thine own were; any man's death diminishes me, because I am involved in Mankind.[171]

God designed relational community to be a safe venue in which the exchange of ideas, inspiration, instruction, and vision could take place. The resourceful partnership with like-minded "veterans of the process" produces opportunity for best practices to survive and new innovations to emerge.

## A Theology of Solidarity

Solidarity assumes a resourceful partnership with colleagues capable of imparting insight and direction essential to the leader's development. Additionally, solidarity becomes

---

[170] Pettit, 115.

[171] Jon Donne, "Meditations XVII," The Quotations Page, http://www.quotationspage.com/collections.html (accessed September 29, 2012).

the social platform from which the leader becomes a part of the community to which he or she seeks to provide leadership. An engaged leader finds a myriad of opportunities germane to his or her context and mission, whereas the isolated leader experiences a dearth of relational connections and minimizes the chances for personal improvement. "Spiritual formation, good or bad, is always profoundly social. You cannot keep it to yourself. Anyone who thinks of it as a merely private matter has misunderstood it."[172] The leader who fails to develop relational connections offers no prospect for the transformative value of solidarity. "The church is to be a haven for healing. People who have gone through a crisis need a refuge, a sanctuary, a safe place—a community that does not dissect, evaluate, or manipulate their souls, but rather allows them to reside with others under God's restorative power."[173] The Apostle Paul admonished the Ephesian church to continue,

> speaking the truth in love ... grow up in all things into Him who is the head—Christ—from whom the whole body, joined and knit together by what every joint supplies, according to the effective working by which every part does its share, causes growth of the body for the edifying of itself in love (Eph. 4:15-16).

He knew effectiveness in the Gospel's proclamation depended upon solidarity within the body of Christ—a resourceful partnership in which every part does its intended share of the overall process.

---

[172] Dallas Willard, *Renovation of the Heart: Putting on the Character of Christ* (Colorado Springs: NavPress, 2002), 182.
[173] Lawrenz, 44.

> *The product of leadership coaching must result in the*
> *transformation of the leader.*

Solidarity enables heightened effectiveness within the body of Christ. That premise of heightened effectiveness presupposes conformity to the image of Christ. As individuals are conformed to Christ with an integrated devotion and within the community, they do not lose their individuality. They are now functioning in a Trinitarian-informed way in which their individuality is expressed in and for the benefit of the Christian community.[174]

Pettit clarifies, "The Hebrew term most often glossed 'community' is *'edah.* The noun *'edah,* 'community, company, assembly' refers to a group of people as a whole, not as a society at large, but as a cohesive community, sharing a common identity and acting in concert."[175] Their sense of community (in the broader sense) provided the foundation for their culture, ideologies, and faith. Through their shared identity, they maintained a relationship rooted in mutual destiny and need.

A more focused sense of solidarity characterizes the spiritual discipline discussed in this segment. It involves the personal connectedness necessary to impact the culture and replicate and encourage maturity traits in emerging leaders. "And the things that you have heard from me among many witnesses, *commit* these to faithful men who will be able to teach others also," (2 Tim. 2:2, emphasis added). "Ministry always involves transmission. It was transmitted from Jesus to Paul and from Paul to Timothy. Now Timothy is given the

---

[174] Paul Pettit, ed., *Foundations of Spiritual Formation: A Community Approach to Becoming Like Christ* (Grand Rapids: Kregel, 2008), 48.
[175] Ibid., 75.

responsibility to transmit it to others who in turn will be faithful in continuing the process."[176] The solidarity required by human agents provides a channel through which God can reveal His will to faithful men and women. The Greek word for "commit" comes from a compound word *paratithimi* (a compound of the words *para* and *tithimi*.)[177] Rener expounds:

> When the words *para* and *tithimi* are compounded together, creating the word *paratithimi*, it means to come close in order to make some type of deposit, like a person who goes to the bank to place a deposit into the repository for safekeeping. Significantly, this is now the word Paul uses when he tells Timothy to "commit" himself to a new group of leaders.[178]

The period of time immediately following the Apostle Paul's dramatic conversion included individuals whose commitment to the solidarity of early believers paved the way for the advancement of the Gospel. If not for the intervention of Early Church leaders on Paul's behalf, possibly one third of the New Testament might not be available to the present canon of Scripture. Paul needed an advocate who could speak with credibility and influence others in his quest to join their ranks. "Spiritual formation is the ongoing process of the triune God transforming the believer's life and character toward the life and character of Jesus Christ—accomplished by the ministry of the Spirit in the context of biblical community."[179] Paul still required

[176] Gary W. Demarest, *The Communicator's Commentary*, The Communicator's Commentary 9 (Waco: Word Books, 1984), 252.

[177] Marvin Richardson Vincent, *Word Studies in the New Testament* (New York: C. Scribner's sons, 1887), 295.

[178] Renner, locations 4386–4392.

[179] Pettit, 24.

someone to walk with him through the initial formation of his spiritual character and clear the debris-laden path of perception toward him. He persecuted the Early Church to such a degree that his reputation preceded him everywhere he went. The intent of his travels prior to his conversion always mandated the arrest and persecution of those whose faith in Jesus Christ ran counter to the established religious system. When he traveled to Jerusalem, the disciples maintained their cautionary stance, not knowing what to expect or if this transformation were, indeed, genuine. I. Howard Marshall reveals, "It was Barnabas who brought Paul to the apostles and related a story which he himself was prepared to believe and which, if true, would fully rehabilitate Paul in the minds of the Christian leaders."[180] Barnabas became the credible reference that allowed Saul to penetrate the inner circle of the same Christians he once persecuted (Acts 9:26-27). John Polhill elaborates,

> The emphasis on Paul as the converted persecutor is first struck in verse 26. On arriving in Jerusalem, Paul attempted to join up with the Christian community there but was at first spurned. Like Ananias, they knew his reputation as persecutor and were not convinced that so vehement an enemy could now be a Christian brother. Barnabas then entered the picture as mediator, his characteristic role in Acts.[181]

Barnabas took Paul to the apostles and testified to his dramatic encounter with Christ and his subsequent

---

[180] I. Howard Marshall, *The Acts of the Apostles: An Introduction and Commentary*, The Tyndale New Testament Commentaries, 1st American ed. (Grand Rapids: Eerdmans, 1980), 175.

[181] John B. Polhill, *Acts*, The New American Commentary 26 (Nashville: Broadman Press, 1992), 243.

conversion from persecutor to preacher. "Barnabas fulfilled his mediating role, securing Paul's acceptance in the apostolic circle."[182]

Solidarity within this context means that Christian community does not depend on what believers have in common in the world but rather what they share in Christ and what they can contribute to the task of equipping new leaders and reaching their cultures (Eph. 4:11-13). The ministry of the Church entails the perfecting (equipping) of the saints. The word for "equipping" used in this verse, *katartismos,*[183] does not appear elsewhere in the New Testament. The directive to perfect the saints carries a weighty commission. It requires the spiritual discipline of solidarity in terms of connectedness with others who share the same ministry goals of reaching a culture and reproducing disciples. Solidarity intends to sharpen the collective effort to accomplish biblically mandated missional goals. While a fellowship of believers must justify its existence by its missional effectiveness, the individual leader must follow a trajectory of personal growth and discipline learning.

God initiated the whole idea of partnership and solidarity when He created humankind. His purposeful act of creation did not reflect experimentation to see what "prototype" could survive. Rather, He deliberately created a human being with whom He might have fellowship. God chose to reveal His plans to other divine beings in heaven (Gen. 1:26-28). His act of inclusiveness demonstrated the value of solidarity and provided an example of the inter-relationship necessary to

---

[182] Ibid.

[183] Francis Foulkes, *The Epistle of Paul to the Ephesians, an Introduction and Commentary*, The Tyndale New Testament Commentaries, 1st ed. (Grand Rapids: Eerdmans, 1963), 120.

accomplish mission. "The 'let us make' thus implicitly extends to human beings, for they are created in the image of one who chooses to create in such a way that shares power with others."[184] God modeled a collective effort in relation to His creation of humans and the establishment of His creative order.

The Apostle Paul used a significant word in his first letter to the church at Corinth. "Let a man so account of us, as ministers of Christ, and stewards of the mysteries of God," (1 Cor. 4:1). He used the word *huperetas*[185] only once in his epistles and it appears in this verse reflecting the Greek word's insightful meaning in reference to those who minister together. This particular Greek word for "ministers" is the word *huperetas*—the word used to depict the lowest class of criminals. Renner further explains,

> A great number of these criminals were held in the bottom galleys of ships. They were seated and chained to a bench along with other criminals—and together they shared common chains, held a common oar, and worked the same number of hours. They all had to provide equal labor to the task. Their entire lives became a group effort. They became inseparable from the other men who were on the bench with them.[186]

Paul implies that a collective effort can only emanate from those locked together in unity and purpose. Solidarity produces joint participation in the venture of mission and interconnectedness that provides mentoring and coaching to leaders intent on being a part of God's purpose and plan.

---

184 Harrelson, 345.
185 Vincent, 205.
186 Renner, locations 15725–15728.

The essence of solidarity connotes an intentional effort to gain and give through the resourceful relationship established between leaders whose intention of personal growth maintains their trajectory. Valuable insight proceeds from peer leadership capable of discerning the Father's heart and integrating those lessons into their personal spiritual development. Spiritual formation's collective effort produces multiple sources skilled in aiding the leader's process of becoming the leader God designed him or her to be.

CHAPTER 7

# The Discipline of Strategy: Staying Intentional

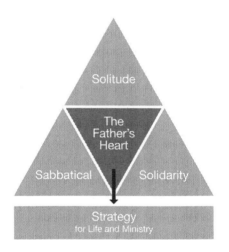

The disciplines of Solitude (staying sensitive), Sabbatical (staying fresh), and Solidarity (staying connected) reside in close proximity to the Father's heart. That resultant proximity produces Strategy (staying intentional). All four components of spiritual formation prove essential in the development of a leader who, in turn, produces leaders. These components characterize the leader who demonstrates intentionality through his or her "real time" example of purpose and connectedness with God's perceived plan.

*Legacies become the product of what leaders leave behind in the lives of those who they lead and in the initiatives they embrace.*

Kouzes and Posner point out "legacies are not the result of wishful thinking. They result from determined doing. The legacy you leave is the legacy you live."[187] Legacies become the product of what leaders leave behind in the lives of those who they lead and in the initiatives they embrace. They become the intangible product of adherence to the disciplines associated with staying in close proximity to the heart of the Father and utilizing the strategy gained there. Together with strategy acquired in the Father's presence, development of the leader's gifts and expansion of his or her gift mix (spiritual gifts, natural abilities, and acquired skills) provides impetus for others to follow with confidence. "There is an important difference between the work that enriches a few at the expense of the many and work that harmonizes and strengthens workers and the communities of which they are a part."[188] Followers do not feel used or insignificant if the strategy of the godly leader emanates from an encounter with God. "Visionary leadership is much more than directing followers. It emanates from within. Leading from within is a way of focusing on our inner knowing and our innate strengths."[189] That leader demonstrates with his or her life a confidence that transmits to others and an inclusiveness that merits approval by those being led.

The spiritual formation of every leader should include the element of strategy that comes form hearing the Father's heart. The leader's resultant actions become intentional. The biblical narrative in Matthew 25:14-30 describes in vivid detail the plight of the individual who fails to develop the talents (or

---

[187] James M. Kouzes and Barry Z. Posner, *A Leader's Legacy* (San Francisco: Jossey-Bass, 2006), 180.

[188] Wirzba, 94.

[189] S. L. Dolan, "Managing by Values: The Leadership Spirituality Connection," *People and Strategy* 35, no. 4 (2012): 25.

gift mix) the master (God) bestows. The passage infers the master's expectancy of increase. The three participants in the parable received differing amounts from the master who expected all three to multiply their holdings. The first two recipients generated a profit while the third simply hid his meager amount in the earth for safekeeping and avoidance of risk. The master praised the first two men but condemned the lack of entrepreneurial effort by the third. His portion found its way into the coffers of the other men, but he was thrown out of their midst.

---

*The spiritual formation of every leader should include the element of strategy that comes form hearing the Father's heart.*

---

Spiritual formation requires leaders to be life-long learners and to work diligently to increase their spiritual, physical, mental, and social skill levels. The position of Strategy requires them to develop the gifts and talents they currently possess and show increase for the master (God). Close proximity to the Father's heart usually reveals creative and innovative ideas toward the development of the leader's gifts. Leaders submit and He stretches them beyond their original limits. A leader's perspective clears and enlarges beyond anything previously imagined. Kouzes and Posner provide a macro perspective of the leader capable of refocusing on the big picture. "When we choose to lead every day, we choose aspirations of long-term significance over short-term measures of success."[190]

A gap between leadership practice and leadership theory

---

[190] Kouzes and Posner, *A Leader's Legacy*, 179.

exists in contemporary leadership culture. John Price contends, "Despite the ever-increasing proliferation of leadership texts, the chasm between leadership theory and practice remains expansive."[191] This chapter intends to clarify that the position of close proximity to the Father's heart produces an intentional application of what the Father chooses to impart and to minimize or eliminate the gap between theory and practice. That impartation becomes the essence of applicable leadership in the lives of leaders who maintain the essential proximity to His heart. The effective leader cannot lead from a theoretical understanding of God or His intent for His servants. He or she must allow God to first shape him or her and then, in concert with the Father, seek to invest in the lives of other leaders.

Greg Atkinson suggests, "If we are intentional about what we do and don't do and strategic about who we delegate to, empower, and free up to lead and take risks, we can…get to watch others get to use their gifts and talents for God's glory, too."[192] The essential truth of this statement reflects the axiom that a leader cannot give what he or she does not have. In order to give, the leader must first receive from God. Henry Blackaby and Richard Blackaby posit,

> One of the issues regarding spiritual leadership is whether spiritual leaders can take people where they themselves have not been. That depends on one's definition of spiritual leadership. If spiritual leadership involves taking people to a location or completing a task, then leaders can lead people to places they have

---

[191] Price, 13.

[192] Greg Atkinson, "Are You an Intentional Leader?" Church Leaders, http://www.churchleaders.com/pastors/pastor-articles/150293-the-intentional-and-strategic-leader.html (accessed August 5, 2013).

not been. But if the goal of spiritual leadership is a more intimate relationship with God, then leaders will never move their people beyond where they have gone themselves.[193]

Leaders who invest in other leaders realize that they have nothing to impart if they neglect personal time spent with God. Greg Waddell believes the leader must be willing to dedicate the time necessary to "help people reach their potential."[194] That time often comes at great sacrifice to the leader intent on producing leadership qualities in others. He adds,

> Spiritual leadership is expressed through service. Spiritual leaders treat their people as they would want to be treated if they were in the same position in the organization. Great leaders must first serve others and this simple fact is central to his or her greatness. True leadership emerges from those whose primary motivation is a desire to help others. In other words, spiritual leaders instill a culture of service throughout the organization, a culture that percolates out to all constituents of the organization.[195]

Leadership and leadership development emanates from both time spent in the presence of the Father and time spent with the individual being developed. A resourceful partnership must characterize the relationship and a strategic

---

[193] Henry Blackaby and Richard Blackaby, *Spiritual Leadership: Moving People on to God's Agenda*, rev. and expanded (Nashville: B & H, 2011), 128.

[194] Greg Waddell, "What is Spiritual Leadership, Anyway?" Lead Strategic, entry posted March 15, 2013, http://leadstrategic.com/2013/03/15/3470/ (accessed August 5, 2013).

[195] Ibid.

understanding of the goal must guide the progress. Ron Cacioppe defines the successful leader who involves himself or herself in the process of developing another leader and then working together as a team to achieve the intended results. "Successful leaders are sensitive to the situation and their followers, are flexible, and able to adapt to the situation to ensure that the vision is achieved"[196] While the mission and the vision may vary, the development of the potential leader needs an intentional investment by a leader whose leadership has been authenticated by time spent with the Father.

---

*Leadership and leadership development emanates from both time spent in the presence of the Father and time spent with the individual being developed.*

---

The purpose of Strategy reveals the possibilities from God's perspective. Leaders cannot know those possibilities until they gain close proximity to Him. The horizons explode with new ventures and opportunities for leaders intent upon becoming all God designed them to be. Strategy's process includes primary alignment with God's revealed will and secondary alignment with His plan for each individual. Personal growth becomes a non-negotiable decision that compels the individual toward excellence in ministry and leadership. Kouzes and Posner further posit, "…leaders have to turn their followers into leaders, and leaders also have to be willing to become followers themselves."[197] Without a strategy, forward progress yields momentum to the gravity of complacency and the spiritual formation of leaders loses its

---

[196] Ron Cacioppe, "Leadership Moment by Moment!" *Leadership & Organization Development Journal* 18, no. 7 (1997): 335.

[197] Kouzes and Posner, *A Leader's Legacy*, 179.

traction. Personal leadership strategy must always originate in close proximity to the Father's heart. Apart from the disciplines of solitude, sabbatical, and solidarity, strategy only takes a familiar and over-used shape and offers nothing of real significance.

Effective leadership aims to live a life in harmony with the Father's heart and, by example, to impart that truth to others and find one's way into the presence of the Father and go there often. James Wilhoit explains, "All persons are formed spiritually. It may be in either a positive or negative direction. This may involve the cultivation of virtues that promote trust in God and foster social compassion or may leave persons wary, self-protective, and unable to promote the welfare of society."[198] The goal of leadership replication should aim to help emerging leaders realize the long-term implications of responding to God's call upon their lives. The process plays out in "real time" and demands disciplines associated with positive spiritual development.

While finishing well should characterize the intentions of the effective leader, Richard Clinton identifies several barriers to finishing well: (1) finances—its use and abuse, (2) the abuse of power, (3) pride, (4) sexual misconduct, (5) family relationships, (6) plateauing, (7) emotional wounding and psychological burnout, and (8) busyness or drivenness.[199] This project asserts that barriers to finishing strong can be minimized or eliminated through intentional adherence to the essential components of a leader's spiritual formation— Solitude, Sabbatical, Solidarity, and Strategy.

The product of Strategy needs no declaration or

---

[198] Jim Wilhoit, *Spiritual Formation as If the Church Mattered: Growing in Christ through Community* (Grand Rapids: Baker Academic, 2008), 17.

[199] Clinton and Leavenworth, *Living and Leading Well*, 10.

introduction. Successful planning ensures a product whose discernable impact produces leaders who hear from God and followers willing to experience personal growth. Strategic leaders raise their level of leadership, demonstrate good stewardship of their talents, and more closely align with God through the discipline of proximity.

## A Theology of Strategy

As the leader devotes his or her development to the spiritual disciplines of Solitude, Sabbatical, and Solidarity, the fourth discipline of Strategy emerges. Only through an intentional effort in the first three disciplines can the product of Strategy be realized. Unfortunately, as Wirzba points out, "A considerable amount of the work performed today, in terms of both the manner and the objectives of the work, does not bring honor to God or facilitate mutual delight."[200] Wendell Berry succinctly adds, "To work without pleasure and affection, to make a product that is not both useful and beautiful, is to dishonor God, nature, the thing that is made, and whomever it is made for. This is blasphemy: to make shoddy work of the work of God."[201] The leader's strategic impact can only gain depth and significance if time spent in solitude, sabbatical and solidarity characterizes his or her regimen of spiritual formation. Otherwise, the Father's discernable will cannot be transmitted to His Church and a predictable default to familiar practices replaces spiritual strategy. The effective leader must gauge his or her strategy by a consistent determination to gain from time spent with the Father.

---

[200] Wirzba, 95.
[201] Wendell Berry, *The Art of the Commonplace: The Agrarian Essays of Wendell Berry* (Washington, DC: Shoemaker & Hoard, 2002), 312.

The Gospel of John identifies the leader's need to remain close to Christ as the qualifying trait for strategic living. "I am the vine, you are the branches. He who abides in Me, and I in him, bears much fruit; for without Me you can do nothing," (15:5). Robertson avows that effective strategy in serving Christ and living a victorious life must originate in a deep sense of love for Him. He explains the Greek phrase, "*(ekeinos estin ho agapon me)* - emphatic use of the demonstrative pronoun *ekeinos*, 'that is the one who loves me,' (14:21). The unseen and Risen Christ will be a real and spiritual Presence to the obedient and loving believer."[202] Love for Christ cannot gain authentic expression if the leader neglects time spent with the Father. Spiritual strategy yields to complacent application of theory and loses the vitality associated with having been in the Father's presence.

*The leader's strategy in life and ministry must correlate with how he or she perceives their calling and how they connect with God's bigger picture.*

William Placher discusses the pursuit of the leader's understanding of the strategy related to his or her calling or vocation as part of something attached to a larger picture of life and ministry and having effects in a much larger sphere of influence. The leader's strategy in life and ministry must correlate with how he or she perceives their calling and how they connect with God's bigger picture. He explains,

Down through the centuries, Christians have looked for definitions of "vocation" somewhere between the trivial sense of "just a job" and the hard-to-believe image of a

---

[202] Robertson, 254.

miraculous voice from heaven. Central to the many Christian interpretations of vocation is the idea that there is something—my vocation or calling—God has called me to do with my life, and my life has meaning and purpose at least in part because I am fulfilling my calling. … If the God who made us has figured out something we are supposed to do, however—something that fits how we were made, so that doing it will glorify God, serve others, and be most richly ourselves—then life stops seeming so empty: my story has meaning as part of a larger story, ultimately shaped by God.[203]

*Everyone's life has meaning and purpose but not everyone understands how to align with God's purpose for his or her life.*

The resulting strategy for life and ministry realizes the potentially far-reaching impact of a leader's input to a community of both believers and leaders. While dialogue addressing various insights concerning "calling" exists, the leader must approach his or her present state as opportunity to facilitate spiritual development in others and articulate the value of God's larger picture.

Everyone's life has meaning and purpose but not everyone understands how to align with God's purpose for his or her life. Effective leaders should strategize to help people connect with God's plan for their lives and understand the significance of their work and its potential impact on their communities. "Through our work we give expression to what (if anything) we love and admire, respect

[203] William Placher, *Callings: Twenty Centuries of Christian Wisdom on Vocation* (Grand Rapids: Eerdmans, 2005), 2–3.

and yearn for. There is an important difference between the work that enriches a few at the expense of the many and work that harmonizes and strengthens workers and the communities of which they are a part."[204]

> *God knew how each potential leader might respond to His call upon his or her life. He uniquely gifted them but left the responsibility for development of their gifts to them.*

As God created humanity, "in His own image" (Gen. 1: 27), He also created them with individually unique qualities. "In truth, we cannot become anything other than who we already are, if we wish to be fulfilled in our lives and vocation. We must stop trying to 'become' something else, or to 'develop' or 'cultivate' some trait that we fundamentally lack, and instead start being who we already are by identifying our giftedness and living it out."[205] God knew how each potential leader might respond to His call upon his or her life. He uniquely gifted them but left the responsibility for development of their gifts to them. If the product of their work and life's application becomes beneficial to the greater community in which they either live or minister, strategic development of their gifts must be placed within the crucible of development.

God knew in advance the eventual response of men and women responding to the gospel's call to full-time service. "For whom He foreknew, He also predestined to be

---

[204] Wirzba, 94.
[205] Arthur F Miller, *The Power of Uniqueness: How to Become Who You Really Are* (Grand Rapids: Zondervan, 2002), 98.

conformed (*symmorphous*)[206] to the image of His Son, that He might be the firstborn among the brethren" (Rom. 8:29). The leader's response to God's call requires a personal and discernable progression of conformity to Christ's image. "Here the new creation, a community of men and women conformed to the image of Christ, is seen to have been from the beginning the object of God's foreknowledge and foreordaining mercy."[207] An intentional effort (strategy) to submit to that process facilitates "a kind of change that is not merely a slight alteration or dressing up of human nature, but rather utter transformation."[208] Effectual leadership emanates from the deliberate effort of integrating the essential components of Solitude, Sabbatical, Solidarity, and Strategy into self-leadership and produces a leader capable of rightly discerning the voice of God amidst the myriad of voices clamoring for the leader's attention.

The Apostle Paul exhorts the congregants of the church in Corinth to maintain their forward motion in their pursuit of the promised prize. "Do you not know that those who run in a race all run, but one receives the prize? Run in such a way that you may obtain it" (1 Cor. 9:24). The word *katalambano*[209] means, "to grab hold of, to seize, to wrestle, to pull down, and to finally make a desired object your very own."[210] Renner elaborates:

Paul uses this word *katalambano* to depict the attitude of a runner who is running with all his energy, straining

---

[206] Vincent, 96.

[207] F. F. Bruce, *The Epistle of Paul to the Romans: An Introduction and Commentary*, The Tyndale New Testament Commentaries 6 (Leicester, England: IVP, 1983), 176.

[208] Lawrenz, 143.

[209] Vincent, 235.

[210] Renner, locations 5010–5017.

forward as he keeps his focus fixed on the finish line. At last the runner reaches the goal, and the prize is now his! He gave that race all he had to give, and it paid off! Had he approached the race with a casual, lazy attitude, the prize would have gone to another. But because he ran to obtain that prize, in the end that's exactly what he did![211]

The runner's strategy requires the exertion associated with reaching deeper into his or her inner being for the fortitude to rise above normally expected results. It represents his or her ultimate effort to seize the prize. While the runner's training yields an ability to compete for the prize, he or she must add a dimension also available to the other contestants. That dimension can only come from a deeper level of training and preparation for the main event and can only be realized in the runner's competition effort.

---

*Effectual leadership emanates from the deliberate effort of integrating the essential components of Solitude, Sabbatical, Solidarity, and Strategy into self-leadership and produces a leader capable of rightly discerning the voice of God amidst the myriad of voices clamoring for the leader's attention.*

---

Likewise, the spiritual leader can only be victorious through an intentional Strategy to apply lessons learned in Solitude, Sabbatical, and Solidarity. His or her uniqueness and giftedness becomes an integral part of God's plan for their lives and the lives He intends to impact through them. The glue that holds together the whole premise of the Proximity

---

[211] Ibid.

Factor is the *leader's determination to remain in close proximity to the heart of the Father* so they can rightly discern the correct course through the myriad of decisions they will need to make on a daily basis.

Adherence to the spiritual discipline of strategy solidly enhances the probability of becoming a champion in life's contest and remains a constant in the life of the leader intent not just on finishing the race, but finishing it as a victor. The Apostle Paul's warning to the church at Corinth illustrates the importance of maintaining close proximity to the Father's heart. He reveals, "But I discipline my body and bring it into subjection, lest, when I have preached to others, I myself should become disqualified," (1 Cor. 9:27). Kenneth Chafin expands the idea of keeping in check all the possibilities of an uncontrolled carnal nature. "The advice is needed by each of us, because one of the great temptations of life is to handle the sacred things of God until we forget that we are clay. It's at that time that we are most vulnerable to temptation."[212] Paul's revelation of his personal struggle with his carnal nature underscores the probability that every human being will at one time or another face his or her soul's nemesis in a contest for supremacy.

Successful leaders remain resolute in their determination to be strategic in their quests for God's approval and to emerge victorious and faithful leaders whom God can trust with His plan.

---

[212] Kenneth Chafin, *The Communicator's Commentary*, The Communicator's Commentary 7 (Waco: Word Books, 1985), 121.

# CHAPTER 8

# The Stewardship of Our Calling

I enjoy the spring and summer—yes, even the heat. I enjoy watching things grow and the beauty produced by the process. I am reminded that I am *involved* in that process. I can especially enjoy it if I stay ahead of the pesky weeds. All it takes for the garden-keeping effort to fail is a lack of attention to the subtle things (weeds) that peek above the ground and begin to emerge into full-grown threats to the healthy plants. If I do not uproot them while they are small, they grow by taking the nutrients intended for the healthy plants and rather become a healthy invader. Soon, all I can see is weeds and my intention of producing something of health and beauty gets lost somewhere in the vegetation.

The purpose in sharing this analogy of the garden links with my earlier teaching (Chapter 5) on the importance of our garden time with the Father. If we do not protect that time, other things will steal it from us and all we will have to show for it is a life of weeds. Maintenance is far better than having to start over again.

My prayer for every pastor and leader is that God will give them the desires of their hearts as their desires please Him. It is not wrong to desire a productive ministry and to actually be happy doing it. But the difficulty in His granting our heart's desire is that we need first of all to be good stewards of what He has entrusted to us. That will require pulling weeds and making sure that nothing interferes with the process wherein the Father seeks to develop us into something of purpose and beauty.

I enjoy reading through the book of Nehemiah and seeing the parallels in the life of one God called for a specific task and the life of the leader intent on responding to what he or she perceives as a call of God upon their life. Just like Nehemiah, if He called us, He will supply us and keep us safe. That part is up to Him. But our growth and eventual emergence into usefulness in God's kingdom depends upon our stewardship of the call. *That* part is up to us.

Leaders can evaluate their calling's stewardship by asking themselves several questions:

1. *How have I regarded my calling?* Do I hold it over His head that I could have done something else and been more successful? Am I inwardly angry that God has not blessed me more? Did I really abandon my previous plans or do they keep reminding me of what I could have been if I hadn't been sidetracked by a call to ministry? Do I regard my calling as genuine or simply an emotional response during a time of personal brokenness?

2. *How have I responded to my calling?* Do I regard Biblical education and being mentored as necessary for my personal process of response to God? Am I a life-long learner? Have I done everything necessary to prepare myself for use by God?

3. *How have I refreshed my calling?* Have I become a slave to the urgent and find myself just surviving the grind of ministry? Do I engage in periodic weed-pulling to maintain a healthy perspective of who I am and what God wants to produce through the cultivation of my spiritual garden? Have I truly learned to enter His rest and enjoy time in His presence?

It is incumbent upon leaders to be good stewards of their calling. There are no healthy churches without healthy pastors and leaders. There are several things that a pastor or leader needs to do to gain and maintain spiritual health.

1. *Re-establish the priority of his or her calling.* Once a man or woman knows that God has called them, nothing should deter them from aligning themselves with the priority of that calling. It should take precedence over all other activities except ministry to family. Preparation and commitment must replace pensivity and convenience.

2. *Regain supernatural eyesight.* Supernatural eyesight is the only cure for myopia—a nearsightedness that robs us of perspective. Leaders only gain such a quality of eyesight from being in close proximity to the Father and learning what is in His heart. Eyes of *faith* will then replace eyes of *fate*. The objective here is to see as God sees.

3. *Re-evaluate present activities.* The leader should ask, "Just what am I doing now that I do not need to be doing?" Some leaders content themselves by duct-taping their hands to the endless treadmill of thankless duty—hoping someone will notice and appreciate their great sacrifice for the cause. To be busy is to be spiritual? Not really. To be busy is to be busy. Spiritual leadership comes from aligning oneself with God's master plan—not trying to *write* it *for* God. Sooner or later, every leader must evaluate whether or not they are leading or just taking a walk.

4. *Release harmful self-concept.* The man or woman of God is not a worm. They are indivivuals whom God has chosen and whom God has validated by nature of His

calling. They are not destined to live in a poverty vow nor are they required to sacrifice their family upon the altar of minsitry. God has set them apart from others and anointed with an high and holy calling.

5. *Revelation through humility.* The key to obtaining God-given favor is to possess a clean heart that is humble before God. God gives grace and favor to the humble. Doors swing open wide and opportunities abound when heaven sees a heart that is broken and utterly dependent upon the Father. Once favor is imparted and influence multiplied, the task is to remain humble.

Leaders possess a special place in God's heart. He loves to bless them. He watches how they respond to His blessing—knowing some will refuse His provision and others will gratefully accept it. The whole purpose of this book is to provide pastors and leaders an understanding of God's purpose in their lives. The Proximity Factor metric illustrates how effectiveness can emerge only from the leader in close proximity to the Father's heart.

---

*The disciplines of **Solitude** (staying sensitive), **Sabbatical** (staying fresh), and **Solidarity** (staying connected) reside in close proximity to the Father's heart. That resultant proximity produces **Strategy** (staying intentional). All four components of spiritual formation prove essential in the development of a leader who, in turn, produces other leaders. These components characterize the leader who demonstrates intentionality through his or her "real time" example of purpose and connectedness with God's perceived plan.*

---

# CHAPTER 9

# The Proximity Factor Self Evaluation

**Definitions:**

**Proximity**: Proximity is simply the relative position of one object (or person) to another. Merriam Webster defines proximity as, "the quality or state of being proximate: closeness."[213] The reference to proximity in this context is in direct relation to one's state of closeness to the Father's heart.

**Solitude**: Solitude in this context refers to time spent alone with God and receives the protection of top priority. Within this context, God does not need to compete with external demands or activities.

**Sabbatical**: A regularly scheduled time of deliberate rest and disconnect from pressures germane to one's calling or vocation.

**Solidarity**: Solidarity exists within the resourceful community of like-minded leaders who trust the relational aspect of collaboration with people capable of speaking into their lives and who, in turn find proximity to the Father's heart a requirement for effective life and leadership. Solidarity is the capability of allowing a select network of mentors and coaches to speak into one's life.

---

[213]Noah Webster, *The Merriam-Webster Dictionary*. (New York: Pocket Books, 1977).

**Strategy**: The intentional action plan produced by time spent in proximity to the Father's heart. Strategy for life and ministry is the result of one's disciplines of solitude, sabbatical and solidarity and the benefits of having been in close proximity to the Father's heart.

**Instructions:**
The questionnaire is divided into four parts – Solitude, Sabbatical, Solidarity, and Strategy. The questions in each section require a numeric response with 1 being lowest and 5 being highest.

Circle the correct response—not as you feel it *should* be but how it really is right now. Be truthful. Enter your scores on the end-chart. Each quarter (weeks 1, 13, 26, and 52) you will be able to compare your scores with previous quarters.

The honesty with which you evaluate yourself gauges the progress in your spiritual formation and self-leadership.

# Solitude:

1. I understanding the importance of solitude as a spiritual discipline.

| Strongly Agree | Agree | Undecided | Disagree | Strongly Disagree |
|---|---|---|---|---|
| 5 | 4 | 3 | 2 | 1 |

2. I understand that the goal of solitude is to hear from God.

| Strongly Agree | Agree | Undecided | Disagree | Strongly Disagree |
|---|---|---|---|---|
| 5 | 4 | 3 | 2 | 1 |

3. I have a regular **time** when I practice solitude.

| Very Frequently | Frequently | Occasionally | Rarely | Never |
|---|---|---|---|---|
| 5 | 4 | 3 | 2 | 1 |

4. I have a regular **place** where I practice solitude.

| Very Frequently | Frequently | Occasionally | Rarely | Never |
|---|---|---|---|---|
| 5 | 4 | 3 | 2 | 1 |

5. I view solitude as important to my spiritual life and leadership.

| Very Important | Important | Moderately important | Of Little Importance | Unimportant |
|---|---|---|---|---|
| 5 | 4 | 3 | 2 | 1 |

# Sabbatical:

1. I understand the importance of sabbatical living as a spiritual discipline.

| Strongly Agree | Agree | Undecided | Disagree | Strongly Disagree |
|---|---|---|---|---|
| 5 | 4 | 3 | 2 | 1 |

2. I understand that the goal of sabbatical living is to gain a life rhythm of rest.

| Strongly Agree | Agree | Undecided | Disagree | Strongly Disagree |
|---|---|---|---|---|
| 5 | 4 | 3 | 2 | 1 |

3. I have a regular **time** when I practice sabbatical.

| Very Frequently | Frequently | Occasionally | Rarely | Never |
|---|---|---|---|---|
| 5 | 4 | 3 | 2 | 1 |

4. I have a regular **place** where I practice sabbatical.

| Very Frequently | Frequently | Occasionally | Rarely | Never |
|---|---|---|---|---|
| 5 | 4 | 3 | 2 | 1 |

5. I view sabbatical as important to my spiritual life and leadership.

| Very Important | Important | Moderately important | Of Little Importance | Unimportant |
|---|---|---|---|---|
| 5 | 4 | 3 | 2 | 1 |

# Solidarity:

1. I understand the importance of solidarity as a spiritual discipline.

| Strongly Agree | Agree | Undecided | Disagree | Strongly Disagree |
|---|---|---|---|---|
| 5 | 4 | 3 | 2 | 1 |

2. I have a network of people and/or friends I allow to speak into my life.

| To a Great Extent | Frequently | Somewhat | Very Little | Not at All |
|---|---|---|---|---|
| 5 | 4 | 3 | 2 | 1 |

3. I integrate insights shared by others in my network.

| Very Frequently | Frequently | Occasionally | Rarely | Never |
|---|---|---|---|---|
| 5 | 4 | 3 | 2 | 1 |

4. I regularly meet with a mentor or coach.

| Very Frequently | Frequently | Occasionally | Rarely | Never |
|---|---|---|---|---|
| 5 | 4 | 3 | 2 | 1 |

5. I consider solidarity important to my spiritual life and leadership.

| Very Important | Important | Moderately important | Of Little Importance | Unimportant |
|---|---|---|---|---|
| 5 | 4 | 3 | 2 | 1 |

# Strategy:

1. I understand the importance of strategy as a spiritual discipline.

| Strongly Agree | Agree | Undecided | Disagree | Strongly Disagree |
|---|---|---|---|---|
| 5 | 4 | 3 | 2 | 1 |

2. My strategy reflects time spent in solitude, sabbatical and solidarity.

| Strongly Agree | Agree | Undecided | Disagree | Strongly Disagree |
|---|---|---|---|---|
| 5 | 4 | 3 | 2 | 1 |

3. My strategy is often influenced by the expectation of others.

| Very Frequently | Frequently | Occasionally | Rarely | Never |
|---|---|---|---|---|
| 5 | 4 | 3 | 2 | 1 |

4. My strategy is clear-cut and intentional.

| Very Frequently | Frequently | Occasionally | Rarely | Never |
|---|---|---|---|---|
| 5 | 4 | 3 | 2 | 1 |

5. I consider strategy important to my spiritual life and leadership.

| Very Important | Important | Moderately important | Of Little Importance | Unimportant |
|---|---|---|---|---|
| 5 | 4 | 3 | 2 | 1 |

The Proximity Factor

| Discipline: | Self Assessment Questions: | Week of Year: | | | |
|---|---|---|---|---|---|
| **Solitude** | | 1 | 13 | 26 | 52 |
| | I understanding the importance of solitude as a spiritual discipline | | | | |
| | I understand that the goal of solitude is to hear from God. | | | | |
| | I have a regular **time** when I practice solitude. | | | | |
| | I have a regular **place** where I practice sabbatical. | | | | |
| | I view solitude as important to my spiritual life and leadership. | | | | |
| **Sabbatical** | | | | | |
| | I understand the importance of sabbatical living as a spiritual discipline. | | | | |
| | I understand that the goal of sabbatical living is to gain a life rhythm of rest. | | | | |
| | I have a regular **time** when I practice sabbatical. | | | | |
| | I have a regular **place** where I practice sabbatical. | | | | |
| | I view sabbatical as important to my spiritual life and leadership. | | | | |

| Solidarity | | 1 | 13 | 26 | 52 |
|---|---|---|---|---|---|
| | I understand the importance of solidarity as a spiritual discipline. | | | | |
| | I have a network of people and/or friends I allow to speak into my life. | | | | |
| | I integrate insights shared by others in my network. | | | | |
| | I regularly meet with a mentor or coach. | | | | |
| | I consider solidarity important to my spiritual life and leadership. | | | | |
| **Strategy** | | | | | |
| | I understand the importance of strategy as a spiritual discipline. | | | | |
| | My strategy reflects time spent in solitude, sabbatical and solidarity. | | | | |
| | My strategy is often influenced by the expectation of others. | | | | |
| | My strategy is clear-cut and intentional. | | | | |
| | I consider strategy important to my spiritual life and leadership. | | | | |

## ABOUT THE AUTHOR

Dr. Jim Beaird is the Regional Executive Director for the Southeast Region of Open Bible Churches, which includes seven states. He pastored for 30 years in Wyoming, Colorado and Iowa before moving to Florida in 2002. He does leadership coaching and consultation and has a heart for pastors and leaders to train them to be true to their calling. He stresses the importance of being life-long learners so a leader can finish life's course with a strong and vibrant effort.

He and his wife, Kris, have three married sons. They reside in the Tampa Bay area. He enjoys the beach, target shooting, riding his Triumph cycle, and golf.